ISBN 978-1-331-83380-2
PIBN 10239799

This book is a reproduction of an important historical work. Forgotten Books uses
state-of-the-art technology to digitally reconstruct the work, preserving the original format
whilst repairing imperfections present in the aged copy. In rare cases, an imperfection in
the original, such as a blemish or missing page, may be replicated in our edition. We do,
however, repair the vast majority of imperfections successfully; any imperfections that
remain are intentionally left to preserve the state of such historical works.

1 MONTH OF FREE READING

at

www.ForgottenBooks.com

By purchasing this book you are eligible for one month membership to ForgottenBooks.com, giving you unlimited access to our entire collection of over 700,000 titles via our web site and mobile apps.

To claim your free month visit:

www.forgottenbooks.com/free239799

English
Français
Deutsche
Italiano
Español
Português

www.forgottenbooks.com

Mythology Photography **Fiction**
Fishing Christianity **Art** Cooking
Essays Buddhism Freemasonry
Medicine **Biology** Music **Ancient**
Egypt Evolution Carpentry Physics
Dance Geology **Mathematics** Fitness
Shakespeare **Folklore** Yoga Marketing
Confidence Immortality Biographies
Poetry **Psychology** Witchcraft
Electronics Chemistry History **Law**
Accounting **Philosophy** Anthropology
Alchemy Drama Quantum Mechanics
Atheism Sexual Health **Ancient History**
Entrepreneurship Languages Sport
Paleontology Needlework Islam
Metaphysics Investment Archaeology
Parenting Statistics Criminology
Motivational

A NIGHT OFF

OR

A PAGE FROM BALZAC

A COMEDY IN FOUR ACTS

(From the German of Schönthan Brothers)

BY

AUGUSTIN DALY

As produced at Daly's Theatre for the first time, Wednesday, March 4th, 1885

Last Copy IF

FITZGERALD PUBLISHING CORPORATION
SUCCESSOR TO
DICK & FITZGERALD
18 Vesey St.,   New York

A NIGHT OFF.

DRAMATIS PERSONAE AND ORIGINAL CAST.

JUSTINIAN BABBITT, *Professor of ancient history in the Camptown university* . . . . MR. JAMES LEWIS

HARRY DAMASK, *his son-in-law* . . . . MR. OTIS SKINNER

JACK MULBERRY, *in pursuit of fortune, under the name of Chumley* . . . . MR. JOHN DREW

LORD MULBERRY, *in pursuit of Jack* . . . . . MR. CHARLES FISHER

MARCUS BRUTUS SNAP, *in pursuit of fame and fortune, under various legitimate aliases* . . . . . . MR. CHARLES LECLERCQ

PROWL, *usher at the university* . . . . MR. F. BOND

MRS. ZANTIPPA BABBITT, *Professor of conjugal management in the Professor's household* . . . . MRS. G. H. GILBERT

NISBE, *the youngest "imp" of the household* . . . MISS ADA REHAN

ANGELICA DAMASK, *the eldest* . . . . . . MISS VIRGINIA DREHR

SUSAN, *the "brassiest"* . . . . MISS MAY IRWIN

MARIA, *servant at Damask's* . . . . MISS JEAN GORDON

TIME.—RECENTLY.   PLACE.—NEAR BY.

TIME OF REPRESENTATION.—TWO HOURS AND A HALF.

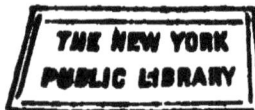

COSTUMES

Prof. Babbitt. Act I. — 1st dress, plain black suit (frock coat), hat and overcoat, all much worn ; 2d dress, dressing-gown substituted for coat; 3d dress, coat resumed, hat. Act II. — Same as 1st dress in Act I. Act III. — Old-fashioned evening clothes, much too large for him ; hat and overcoat for last entrance. Act IV. — Same as Act III.

Damask. Acts I., III., and IV.—Business suit ; derby hat; gloves. Act III. — House-jacket and cap.

Jack. Business suit ; derby hat.

Lord Mulberry. Heavy clothing ; large travelling coat ; muffler ; fur gloves; sealskin cap, etc.

Snap. Acts I. and II. — Very loud clothes, with plenty of jewellery. Fur-trimmed ulster ; silk hat. Act III. — Roman costume under the ulster ; old street gaiters. Act IV. — 1st dress, trousers and coat much too small for him ; Roman breastplate instead of shirt front ; 2d dress, same as in Act I.

Prowl. Plain suit of rusty black.

Mrs. Babbitt. Act I. — Travelling costume. Act II. — Street dress. Act III. — House (dinner) dress. Act IV. — House (morning) dress.

Nisbe. Act I. — Travelling costume. Act II. — Street dress. Act III. — House (dinner) dress ; hat, wrap, and gloves. Act IV. — House (morning) dress.

Angelica. Act I. — Street dress. Act II. — House (morning) dress. Act III. — House (dinner) dress. Act. IV. — House (morning) dress.

Susan. Muslin dress ; linen collar and cuffs ; cap. Hat and shawl in Act III.

Maria. Conventional housemaid's costume, with hat and shawl.

PROPERTIES.

Act. I. — Study-table down L. Smaller table down R. Sofa C., between fireplace and footlights. Curtains at alcove. Lounge and table in alcove. Bookcases, containing books, against walls. Classical busts. Chairs near tables and about stage. Carpet down. Books, papers, writing-materials, postal-card, and a letter containing a small bunch of pressed flowers, on study-table down L. Books, pamphlets, newspapers, etc., on small table down R. Easy-chair at fireplace. Easel, with portrait, R. Table near C. Cabinet containing silverware, small boxes, jewel-cases, etc. Pack of cards in drawer of table R. Portfolio on table R. Scrap-basket near table L. Ornaments on L. table. Footstool. Dusting-cloth and feather-duster for Susan. Load of copy-books for Prowl. Spectacles for Professor. Large roll of MSS. in drawer of L. table. Umbrella for Susan. Eyeglass for Snap. Four photographs (one of them an *opéra bouffe* character) in pocket of Snap's ulster. Satchels and hand-baggage for Mrs. Babbitt. Flowers, satchels, etc., for Nisbe. Eyeglasses for Mrs. Babbitt.

ACT II. — Carpet down. Writing-table C., with desk-chair in front of it, and an easy-chair near by at L. Chair R. of table. Sofa R. Easy-chair L. Other chairs, and ornaments, pictures, etc., *ad lib.* Bell and writing-materials on table C. Card on tray for MARIA. Leather pocket-book for JACK, containing photograph, small black curl tied with a pink ribbon, crushed rosebud, plain gold ring, package of bills, and pawn-ticket. Hat for JACK to enter with. Magazine for DAMASK. Key in drawer of writing-table. Note for JACK. Atomizer, containing cologne, on table C. Pocket-book, containing a single bill, for PROFESSOR. Watch for DAMASK. Two cigars in paper parcel in PROFESSOR'S pocket. Cigars, in case, for DAMASK. Loose matches in PROFESSOR'S pocket, and matches, in case, for DAMASK. Handkerchief and MSS. for SNAP.

ACT III. — Furnishings used in Act I. Lighted lamps on tables R. and L. Fire in grate C. Band music off stage. Copy of *Life* and bunch of keys for NISBE. Watch for PROFESSOR. MSS. in SNAP'S pocket. Ticket for JACK. Sheet of paper, written, for SNAP. Duster for SUSAN. Pen, in holder, and tickets for PROFESSOR. Work-baskets and fancy-work for MRS. BABBITT and ANGELICA. Hat and overcoat for PROFESSOR. Hat for DAMASK on table near C. Door-bell off L. C. Pocket-book and contents used in Act II. Small medicine vial for MRS. BABBITT. Tea and tea-service for SUSAN. Roman costume for SNAP to wear under ulster.

ACT IV. — Furniture, bric-a-brac, etc., as per Act I. Large rug for SNAP. Tray, with breakfast, for SUSAN. Large valise for NISBE. Basket for SUSAN. Watch for JACK. Valise, half filled, for PROFESSOR. Wear-ing-apparel in alcove up R. C. Watch for MULBERRY. Clothes-basket, nearly full of knickknacks, for SUSAN.

ABBREVIATIONS.

In observing, the player is supposed to face the audience. C. means centre; R., right; L., left; R. C., right of centre; L. C., left of centre; C. D., centre door; R. D., right door; L. D., left door; D. R. C., door right of centre; D. L. C., door left of centre; D. F., door in the flat; C. D. F., centre door in the flat; R. D. F., right door in the flat; L. D. F., left door in the flat; I G., 2 G., 3 G., etc., first, second, or third grooves, etc.; I. E, 2 E., 3 E., etc., first, second, or third entrances, etc.; R. U. E., right upper entrance; L. U. E., left upper entrance; UP, up stage or toward the rear; DOWN, down stage or toward the audience; X., means to cross the stage; X. R., cross toward the right; X. L., cross toward the left.

	R. C.	C.	L. C.	L.

C.

A NIGHT OFF;

OR,

A PAGE FROM BALZAC.

ACT I.

SCENE. — The PROFESSOR'S *Study. At back* C., *a mantel and fireplace. At* R. C., *an alcove which can be closed with a curtain, backed by a window, and reached by a step or two. At* L. C., *general entrance to the apartment. Doors,* R. *and* L. *Down* L. *a study-table, full of books, papers, etc. Down* R. *a smaller table with books, etc., newspapers and pamphlets. A sofa at* C., *between fire and front. A lounge and table in the alcove. Bookcases against the walls, classical busts, etc.*

The curtain rises to a very bustling air, and SUSAN *is discovered wiping the dust from the furniture with a cloth, her duster under her arm. READY* PROWL, *to enter* L. C.

SUSAN. Not much of a job to dust the house when missus is away. The Professor wouldn't know if the dust was an inch thick on everything. (*Picks up a folded country news-paper.*) Here's the morning paper not opened. Let's see what's in it. (*Leans against table as she opens the paper. Suddenly gives a start.*) Oh, my! Here's a start. (*Reads.*) "Opera House. Special Announcement. The Grandest Combination of Dramatic Talent in the World. The under-signed respectfully announces the appearance of the renowned

.5.

Central Park Combination in a series of their brilliant per-
formances, pronounced by press and public the *ne plus ultra*
of dramatic representations." (*Speaks.*) Gracious! don't that
sound splendid? (*Reads.*) "The management guarantees
that each performer in this Matchless Troupe is an ac-
knowledged Star — the whole forming a galaxy of histrionic
constellations. Having recently concluded a brilliant engagement at the New York Central Park Casino before the
wealth and culture of the Metropolis, will appear before the
discriminating and intelligent public of this far-famed University Centre, on Monday evening, March 1st, and every
evening until further notice. Each performance will be
under the personal supervision of the public's most obedient
servant, Marcus Brutus Snap, Manager. For particulars,
see programmes. No connection with any other combination on the road." (*Speaks.*) Well! I know this much.
While Mrs. Babbitt's away, I'll go to the theatre every night.
Catch her letting me out if she was home! (*Puts paper on
table,* L.)

PROWL, *a severe man, ENTERS with a load of copy-books.*

PROWL (L., *in surly tone*). Professor in?
SUSAN (*puts paper down*). Be back presently. What have
you got there?
PROWL. Composition books. Fourth class. Fifty-two of
'em. (*Puts them on table, crosses to* R.)
SUSAN. And when have we got to look over them?
PROWL. By day after to-morrow.
                    [*READY* PROFESSOR, *to enter* L. C.
SUSAN (*crosses to* L. *table, opens one of the books and
reads*). "The Second Punic War." Great jiminy! The
Professor will shudder when he sees 'em. Say, do you
know, these Punic Wars generally strike us every year about
the same time, just as we are pickling cucumbers?
PROWL. *It's the* everlasting round that drives me mad.

The boy, like history, repeats himself. I hate boys. I've been usher twenty-five years, and I hates 'em. I have dreams in which I cuts off millions of 'em at a blow.

SUSAN (*who has been looking over a book*). Did you ever hear such a dunce? Listen to what this chap writes: "The First Punic War having finished in the year 241 B.C., the Second Punic War commenced in the year 218 B.C., or just 23 years after." Now, did you ever! As if the year 218 could come after the year 241! (*Slams book on the pile. Crosses to* R.)

PROWL. I wish that was the worst they did.

The PROFESSOR *ENTERS from the street,* L. C., *in hat and overcoat. Both much worn. He wears gold spectacles.*

PROFESSOR (C.). Now, Prowl! What brings you here?

PROWL (L.). Brought the composition books. (*Points to them.*)

PROF. (*assisted by* SUSAN *in removing his coat*). Oh, very well.

SUSAN (R.). They're full of mistakes, too.

PROF. Indeed! (*Gives her his hat and coat.*)

SUSAN. And the umbrella?

PROF. What umbrella?

SUSAN. Oh, dear! The new silk one, Professor. I reminded you not to leave it behind you again.

PROF. (C., *uneasily*). Have I really —

SUSAN. Of course! What day is this? Wednesday! Ancient history, fifth class, from 2 to 3; first class from 3 to 4. Run and look for it, Mr. Prowl. (*Crosses to* C.)

PROF. It may be in the faculty's room.

PROWL. Very good, Professor.

SUSAN (*calls after him*). Dark brown! The handle shakes a little, and the catch is missing. [PROWL *EXITS.*

PROF. (*who has come down to his writing-table,* L.). No letters from my wife, Susan?

SUSAN.   No, sir.

PROF.   None to-day.   None yesterday.   I hope nothing has happened.

SUSAN.   What could have happened?   Don't worry.

PROF.   Has anybody called?

SUSAN.   Yes, sir; gentleman to see you.   Half an hour ago.

PROF.   Who was it?

[*READY* DAMASK *and* ANGELICA, *to enter* L. C.

SUSAN.   I don't know him.   Odd-looking gentleman. Smooth-shaved face, lots of rings on his hand.   Said he'd call again in half an hour.

PROF.   Very good.   We'll see who it is.

SUSAN.   What shall I cook for supper, sir?

PROF.   Don't bother me about that.   Cook what you please.

SUSAN.   That's what you always say, and when I do you won't touch anything.

PROF. (*with a sigh*).   I have no appetite.

SUSAN.   Of course you haven't.   You study, and write, and work, day and night.   You should take exercise.   Professor, try roller-skating.   (*Struck with idea.*)   But wait till the theatre comes; you shall go every night.

PROF.   The theatre?

SUSAN.   Yes.   Didn't you read the paper?   Here it is. (*Points to paper.*)   Opera House, March 1st.

DAMASK *puts his head in door*, L. C.

DAMASK.   Good-morning, papa!   There's a charming little woman in the next room.   Shall I bring her in?

PROF.   A charming — ?   Oh, you mean your wife.   Certainly, certainly.   (*Gets* R.)

ANGELICA *pushes* DAMASK *aside and looks in.*   SUSAN *EXITS*, L. C.

ANGELICA.   Papa, do you want this horrid creature to come in, too?

PROF. (R.).   Come in, you big, overgrown children; you show yourselves seldom enough to your poor forsaken father.

DAM. (*coming down*. C.).   I know it's wrong, but we are so snug and happy together.

ANG. (L.).   And Harry's away all day —

PROF. (*crosses to* C.).   Of course.   It's right.   It's right.

ANG.   But you should come to see us.

DAM.   What do you do with yourself all alone?

PROF. (C.).   It's dull enough.   I had no idea I should miss your mamma and Nisbe so much.

ANG.   When did you hear from them last?

PROF. (*crosses to* L., *handing her a letter from table*, L.).   Day before yesterday.

ANG. (*opens letter*).   Pressed flowers inside.   How romantic of mamma! (*Takes out a small bunch of pressed flowers.*)

PROF.   Nisbe picked them in her walks. (*Crosses to* C.)

ANG.   So nice. (*Reads letter.*)

DAM. (R.).   So the Springs are doing mamma some good?

PROF. (C.).   Yes; but not me. (*Takes him one side.*)   I say, my dear boy, these watering-places cost a great deal of money.   I've reckoned it up.   I won't get off for less than four hundred and sixty dollars.

DAM. (R.).   But it was really indispensable for your wife's health.

PROF.   And for Nisbe's too.   The girl is twenty, and must be shown about a little.   But you know how closely I have to manage with my salary.   Four hundred and sixty dollars make a big hole in my calculations.   I have bridged it temporarily by drawing on Nisbe's money in the savings bank, but that must be replaced, for if my wife found it out — (*nervously*).

DAM.   It might be unpleasant.

PROF.   I wonder if I ought to risk a little in stocks.

DAM.   Professor — don't think of it.

PROF.   Other people do it.

DAM.   But you know nothing about stocks.

PROF.   That's so.   (*Crosses to* R.)   But there's no money to be made with what I *do* know about.

ANG.   Mamma and Nisbe seem to be enjoying themselves. (*Folding the letter.*)

[*READY* SUSAN, *with umbrella, to enter* L. C.

PROF. (*crosses to* C.).   I don't begrudge 'em, but I have to live like a hermit.

ANG. (L., *rising*).   Poor papa!   What do you do with yourself?

PROF.   I've tried everything.   Put my library in order. Rummaged through my letters and manuscripts as far back as my college days.   (*Crosses to* L.)   Stop! I've unearthed this thing here and really got some pleasure out of it. (*Takes a large roll of MSS. from drawer.*)

DAM. (*crosses to* C., *taking it*).   What is it?   Look's like poetry.

PROF. (L.).   It's worse!   It's a tragedy.

ANG. (R.).   Written by you?

PROF.   Yes; at college.   What student has not written a Roman tragedy.   When I read it over again the other day, I enjoyed it immensely.   Of course it's crude and unfinished, but there's snap in it,

SUSAN *ENTERS*, L. C., *with the umbrella.*

and fire — the fire of youth.   Isn't there, Susan?

SUSAN (*clasping the umbrella to her bosom, and with a heavenward sigh*).   O Professor!

PROF. (*crosses to* DAMASK).   You must know I read it to her.

DAM. *and* ANG. (*laughing*).   Read it to Susan!   Ha, ha, ha!

PROF. (L. C.). Laugh away. I never see you, and a man must read his good things to somebody. So Susan had to suffer.

SUSAN. O Professor! I loved to listen to it. Mr. Harry (*crosses to him*), it's a heavenly piece! But so sad! Oh, *so* sad! (*Wipes her eyes and sobs.*)

PROF. Now don't commence to howl again.

SUSAN (*crying*). I can't help it. If I only see the writing, I must cry. It's just like peeling onions. (*EXITS*, L. C.)

[ANGELICA *takes up a book from table*, R., *and reads.*

PROF. You see how I've degenerated these last four weeks. Reading my youthful donkeyisms to a servant.

DAM. No harm in that. Molière read his plays to his housekeeper. The criticism of an unhackneyed mind —

ANG. (*starting up*). Oh! oh! this is too horrible! (*Goes across to table*, L. *She still carries in her hand the pressed flowers. She also takes over the book she has been reading. Throws herself on seat.*)

PROF. What is it?

DAM. What's the matter?

ANG. O papa! Is the man who wrote this book to be believed?

PROF. (*adjusts his spectacles, and looks at title of book*). Balzac! (*Smiles.*) Well, I believe he's considered a judge of human nature.

ANG. (*throws flowers into basket*). Is he? (*Crosses to* DAMASK.) Then, sir, what have you got to say?

DAM. Say to what?

ANG. There! Please read for yourself. (*Shows an open page.*)

DAM. (R., *reads*). "Every bride that lives — if she could but know the past and secret life of her husband — would renounce him even at the steps of the altar." Well! (*Returns book.*)

ANG. Well? What has your past life been?

DAM. Really, my love —

ANG. Papa, what has his past life been?

PROF. Nonsense!

ANG. (C., *mimicking them*). " Really, my love!" "Nonsense!" You won't get off with that. Here is the book. Confess.

DAM. But I haven't anything to confess.

ANG. Then how could the man make such an assertion?

DAM. Simply, he didn't know *me*, that's all.

ANG. We'll see if you'll be so witty when we get home. You think papa protects here. Good-evening, papa! (*Throws book on table*, L.)

PROF. Going so soon?

DAM. (*crosses to her*). Angelica, listen to reason.

ANG. (*waving him off*). We'll talk it over at home.

[*READY* SUSAN *and* SNAP, *to enter* L. C.

DAM. Nice prospect!

PROF. (*getting* R.). You're both always telling me about your domestic happiness, and every time I see you, you end up in a quarrel.

ANG. (*half crying*). You take his part, do you? Oh, if mamma were only home! I'd soon know everything. (*Goes to door.*)

DAM. Wait for me. I'll go with you.

ANG. Don't trouble yourself. (*EXITS*, L. C.)

DAM. (*after a pause, during which he and the* PROFESSOR *look at each other*). Professor, I don't wish to reproach you, but if *I* ever have a daughter, I'll train her up to place implicit confidence in her husband. (*EXITS*, L. C.)

PROF. Will you? Then you'll have a hard job of it. But I'll take this as a warning. Balzac shall be concealed. If my wife got hold of it, she'd be quite capable of putting conundrums to me. (*Hurries off*, L., *with the book.*)

SUSAN *ENTERS*, L. C.

SUSAN.   Step in here, please.

SNAP *ENTERS*, L. C. ; *wears a fur-trimmed overcoat, and is very loud in style.*

SNAP.   Exactly.   (*Removes hat, which he places on table.*)
SUSAN.   I told the Professor you had called before.
SNAP.   Thanks !   Thanks !
SUSAN (*crosses to* L.).   I'll tell him you've come again.
SNAP.   Just one minute, please.   (*Takes off his overcoat, and lays it on chair with his hat.   Displays a very loud get-up underneath.   Throws his frock coat open, and dangles his eyeglass with a light comedy, but theatrical air.*)   We must get ready for the first entrance.   Have the goodness to say that Mr. Marcus Brutus Snap begs the favor of an interview.
SUSAN (*amazed*).   Mr. Snap !   Lor !   The manager !
SNAP.   You may say to the Professor that I am calling on the most prominent people of the place, and add that I am my own advance agent.   We billed the town last night.
[SUSAN *going.*
Stay !   One word more.   Is the family fond of the drama ?
SUSAN (L.).   Oh, no indeed !   Since I lived here none of 'em ever went to the theatre.
SNAP.   And a — how — how — long have you lived here ?
SUSAN.   Ten years the Fourth of July.
SNAP.   Ten years without the drama !   I have heard that it was a one-night town.   I believe it.   And why — why don't you go to the theatre ?
SUSAN.   Mrs. Babbitt won't allow it.
SNAP.   How about Mr. Babbitt ?
SUSAN.   Oh, he's written a play.
SNAP.   The deuce he has !
SUSAN.   If you don't believe me, there it is on his desk now.   Oh, that's a piece, I can tell you !   It's all about the Romans and the Greeks.
SNAP.   Has it ever been produced ?

SUSAN (*indignantly*). No. Nobody ever seen it even — but me.

SNAP. Ah! (*Meditatively.*)

SUSAN. Sir?

SNAP (*still meditating*). There's more in this.

SUSAN. No, there's no more than this one.

SNAP (*recovering*). I crave your pardon! Stay, another word. The Professor is one of the leading men in the University?

SUSAN. I should think so. When he crosses the street all the boys take off their hats.

[*READY* PROFESSOR, *in dressing-gown, to enter* L. D.

SNAP (R.). So — so. (*Reflectively.*)

SUSAN. What's the matter?

SNAP (*recovering*). Ha! nothing — 'tis the heat.

SUSAN. I'll tell the Professor.

SNAP. That's right.

SUSAN (*going*). Cricky! To think he should come to our house! (*EXIT,* L. *door.*)

SNAP (*natural*). Now, my boy, for a little diplomacy. When we played in Nantucket, two years ago, I worked a little thing like this to perfection. The leading banker of the place had a daughter. The daughter had written a play. I produced it. It was the worst I ever read, but we jammed the house. The old man brought the whole town with him. Then my wife gave it for her benefit, and we sold the house out again. Two crammed houses in one week. Shakespeare couldn't have done it — but the bank did.

The PROFESSOR *ENTERS* L. *door, in a dressing-gown.*

PROF. You wish to see me, I believe?

SNAP (R.). I have taken the liberty of calling to invite your attention to the programme of my company which is about to appear at the Opera House. The district judge, who is now in town, has signified his intention of helping us.

So have the — the — several others ! You know the district judge, of course ? There are five very good seats right alongside the district judge, and I reserved them for your family, in the hope that — that —

PROF. I am very sorry, but we never go to the theatre.

SNAP. You will make an exception with us. We give a varied programme, — "Romeo and Juliet." "Frou-Frou," "7-20-8," "Macbeth" and "Pinafore."

PROF. Variety enough.

SNAP. And we play them, sir, right up ! They go like a greased wheel.

PROF. Really?

SNAP. It's absolutely a star performance. My wife and myself appear in everything. You could wake us up in the middle of the night and we'd give you the whole *répertoire* without a break. As for the company — all artists ! You understand, artists ! My leading young man is a marvel — stepped from the drawing-room to the stage. English, of course ! There's a mystery about him, and a family history — a history and a mystery ! The moment he comes on, you see that you have got the real thing before you.

PROF. (L., *shifting his position uneasily*). Indeed !

SNAP. It's my specialty to find unknown talent. It's the same with authors. I have brought men forward who have made fortunes. Last year in Nantucket — this in confidence — a young lady, of a wealthy family, gave me her maiden effort — a tragedy.

PROF. (*interest*). And you produced it ? (*Indicates a seat.*) Sit down.

SNAP. (*sits eagerly, and draws his chair near* PROFESSOR). I produced it, and it succeeded ! (*Slaps* PROFESSOR's *knee.*) We sold the house out six nights running. My wife played the principal part, and there wasn't a dry eye in the theatre Now they play it everywhere, outside of New York, and the fair author's coining money.

PROF.   Is it possible? (*Very reflectively.*)

SNAP.   It's the solemn fact. (*Rising and putting chair back.*) But I won't detain you ; you are busy.

PROF. (*detains him*).   Not at all, my dear sir.   Pray go on.

SNAP.   No ; I've intruded too long already, and as you don't take any interest in theatricals —

PROF.   Well, I can hardly say that ; you see, I — I — I — have a *friend* who has written a play !

SNAP.   No ! (*Aside.*)   He nibbles.

PROF.   I happen to have the manuscript by me.   (*Points to table.*)   It's a Roman tragedy, founded on the historical incident of the abduction of the Sabine maidens by the Roman warriors.

SNAP.   A Roman tragedy !   The very thing for us.   My company is especially adapted for Roman tragedy, my wife particularly.   Might I beg a glance —

[*READY* SUSAN, *to enter* L. C.

PROF. (*taking up the MSS.*).   I hardly know —

SNAP.   Oh, you may rely on me.   I'm all discretion.   What does he call it ?

PROF. (L.).   " The Beautiful Sabine."

SNAP.   Splendid title !   Immense !   Catching !

PROF.   You think so ?

SNAP.   Oh, superb !   Think of it on a three-sheeter : — " The Beautiful Sabine ! "   Oh, there's draft in that title !   You must let me read it.   I'll take it with me, and bring it back in the morning.

PROF.   No — no — I can't let it out of my hands.

SNAP.   Very good.   We won't quarrel about that.   I'll read it here on the spot — that is, with your permission (*trying to get MSS.*).

PROF.   Well, I don't know how I can —

SNAP.   Put me quietly into a corner for half an hour, and I'll skip right through it.

SUSAN *ENTERS*, L. C.

SUSAN. Professor, there's a gentleman called to see you. I asked his name, and he said, "No matter on second thoughts tell him Mulberry."

[*READY* MULBERRY, *to enter* L. C.

PROF. (L.). "No matter on second thoughts tell him Mulberry"! I don't know any one of that name.

SUSAN. He said, "Tell the Professor it's an old friend of his."

PROF. He's nothing of the kind. What impudence! (*Crosses* C.)

SNAP. Must be a book agent; I recognize the cheek.

PROF. Did you tell him I was in?

SUSAN. I can't tell a lie, Professor, and I did.

PROF. (*sighs*). That being the case, show him up.

SUSAN (*aside*). They've got the play out! Oh, cricky! we'll go to the theatre every night! (*EXITS, crossing to* L. C.)

PROF. If you really insist on glancing over this — ahem — trifle, step in yonder, and draw the curtains; you won't be disturbed. (*Gives MSS. to* SNAP, *and points to alcove,* R. C.)

SNAP. Oh, make me quite at home. No ceremony with me (*going*). (*Aside.*) I'll produce it if it's worse than the banker's daughter's. (*EXITS, up* R. C.)

LORD MULBERRY *ENTERS* briskly, L. C., *muffled in travelling-coat, shawl round throat, big fur gloves, etc.*

MULBERRY (L.). Ah. my dear sir, there you are; I haven't much time to spare — just travelling through, but here I am. (*Grasps both hands.*)

PROF. (*aside*). I never saw the man in my life.

MUL. (*crosses* R., *unwrapping shawl*). I keep my word, you see.

PROF. (*aside*). He's taking off his things. (*Aloud.*) Excuse me, but I really —

MUL. (*pausing in the act of disrobing*). You don't remem ber me?

PROF. To be quite honest about it —

MUL. (*eying him*). Why, Mulberry!

PROF. Mulberry! Ah, to be sure! Mulberry (*aside*), not an idea.

MUL. Let me remind you. You were in New York two years ago.

PROF. Yes; on business.

MUL. I suppose so. I met you at a *matinée*.

PROF. I sometimes —

MUL. So do I. (*Chuckles.*) We sat next each other, and got into conversation. I told you I was an Englishman, and you told me you were an American. I was surprised to hear it, as you speak the language so correctly. You described the hole of a place where you lived, and I said I might call and hunt you up, if I passed through. If it's not agreeable, I'll go. (*Begins to wrap up again.*)

PROF. (*apologetically*). Not at all! not at all!

MUL. Not at all agreeable?

PROF. I mean to say I'm delighted. (*Aside.*) I'm not like Susan, I can tell a lie. (*Aloud.*) Pray, sit down (*They sit.*) I'm only sorry that my wife is not here. She is now at the White Sulphur Springs with my daughter.

MUL. Ah, with Angelica?

PROF. (*astonished*). No; with Sophonisba.

MUL. Oh, the youngest. Angelica was suffering from hay-fever. Is she better?

PROF. Thank you, yes. She is married. (*Aside.*) I must have been very confidential with him.

MUL. (*presses his hand to his head and speaks solemnly*). Is the marriage a happy one?

PROF. Remarkably so. The young people live like tur-tle-doves (*aside*), or did until this afternoon.

MUL. (*crosses to* L. — *strikes table with his clinched fist*). Death and furies!

PROF. (*bounds up*). I beg pardon.

MUL. (*sits, L. To himself, in a passion*). The luck — the blind luck that some people have with their sons and daughters!

PROF. I trust you've had no bad luck with yours.

MUL. (*glares at him*). You actually talk as if I had not told you the whole story.

PROF. (*nervously*). Oh, I remember — your daughter.

MUL. (*savagely*). No; I have no daughter. My son, my son John, the rascal! (*Bangs table.*)

[*READY* SNAP, *to appear behind curtain.*

PROF. Oh, yes! your son John, the rascal!

MUL. (*piteously and half crying*). Things went on just as I told you they would.

PROF. (*bewildered*). You surprise — you alarm me.

MUL. (*crossly*). How can it alarm you? How could they turn out differently? He wouldn't study; he wouldn't go into the army; he would run into debt; he would fall in love with every designing minx, and now he's bolted. (*Brings his fist down again.*) Bolted!

[*The* PROFESSOR *moves the inkstand, etc., out of his way.*
Now I have no son. It's all over.

PROF. (*back to* C.) But such a promising young man —

MUL. Promising! Egad! I couldn't get him to promise. (*Pulling his chair nearer.*) I'll tell you the whole story.

PROF. (*sighs*). Oh, dear!

[SNAP *looks in from behind curtain.*

SNAP. Professor! Professor!

MUL. (*impatient*). What the devil's that?

PROF. (*rises*). Excuse me one moment. (*Goes to* SNAP.) What do you want?

SNAP (*meeting him*). Don't be offended, but I couldn't sit there and contain my joy.

PROF. (*tickled*). Have you read it?

SNAP. I've been through the first act. It's simply grand!

Such a picture of human passion — and the words, the dialogue !

PROF.   You really think it could be performed ?

SNAP.   It would be an outrage, Professor, to leave such a work in the closet.   It belongs to the stage.   To my stage.

PROF.   But I must consider —

MUL. (*bounds up*).   If you're busy, I'll go.

PROF. (*pressing him back into seat, returns*).   No, no.   I'll be at your service in one moment.   (*Back to* SNAP.)   Read the other acts.   They're all better than the first.

SNAP.   No, Professor.   With all respect, they can't be better.   That's simply impossible.   They may be stronger, but they can't be better.   (*Aside.*)   I've got him !   I've got him !   (*Disappears behind curtain.*)

PROF. (*returns to seat*).   Now, my dear sir.   (*He is much elated and rubs his hands.*)

MUL.   Let me see — how much did I tell you that day at the *matinée* ?

PROF.   Well, the fact is that my mind has been so occupied since —

MUL. (*testily*).   Then there's nothing left for me but to go all over it again.

PROF. (*shakes his head*).   No ! no ! no !

MUL.   To make a short story, my wife was a woman of romantic ideas — all poetry, no fortune.   We were married in '48·

PROF.   '48 – '85, thirty-seven years ago.

MUL.   How time passes !   Well, my eldest son was born.

PROF.   Yes, yes ; John, the rascal.

MUL.   No, sir ; Reginald Plantagenet and Victor Cholmondely came before John.   John is the youngest and the worst.

SNAP *RE-ENTERS*.

SNAP.   Gentlemen, I beg a thousand pardons — (*to* PROFESSOR) but I have a question to ask.

PROF. What is it ? (*Without rising.*)

SNAP (*bending down to his ear*). Is there any local military organization in the town, or a fire company, or anything of that sort?

PROF. Why?

SNAP. Well, for the grand procession of priests at the end of the second act. It requires a large supernumerary force, and if we can get a local organization—eh? See?

PROF. I can't possibly say. (*Rises and puts chair back.*)

MUL. (*rising*). I'll call another time. (*Puts chair back.*)

PROF. (*absently*). Any time.

MUL. (*severely*). I am confiding a most important family matter to you, and you let me stand here —

PROF. (*mildly and bewildered*). I'm really very busy at present.

MUL. (*testily*). Do you think I have nothing to do? I must catch the 5–30 express.

[*READY* SUSAN, *to enter* L. C.

PROF. What a pity !

MUL. Pity won't keep this train back. (*Wraps up.*) When I get through in New York, I'll run up again for a day, and I hope (*looking at* SNAP) we shall not be interrupted.

PROF. The very thing. Come when you can. Don't hurry.

MUL. Pray, remember where we left off. I don't want to begin all over again.

PROF. No, no; anything but that.

MUL. Present my regards to your wife, but not a word to her about Jack. I wish the matter kept profoundly secret, for the present. (*Wrings* PROFESSOR'S *hand warmly, wipes away a tear, pats* PROFESSOR'S *shoulder.*) Jack, Jack, why did you bolt! (*EXITS*, L. C.)

PROF. What a man! (*To* SNAP.) I assure you, I haven't the remotest notion who he is! (*Rings bell suddenly and calls.*) Susan !

Susan *ENTERS*, L. C.

SUSAN. Yes, sir.

PROF. (L.). If that gentleman calls again, I'm not at home. I've gone out and won't be back. I've joined an exploring .expedition to the North Pole. You tell him that, and I'll take the consequences.

SUSAN. Very well. I wash my hands of it. (*EXITS*, L. C., *shaking her head.*)

SNAP (R., *who has been turning over the pages of the MSS. at R. table*). Professor, I am willing to stake my reputation on this production. That situation at the end of act third can be worked up to create furious enthusiasm in the audience. Only see ! In front you have the Roman soldiers each with a shrieking maiden in his ruthless grasp. At back, in centre, King Titus Tatius with arms raised to Heaven, invoking a malediction on the foe. At that instant the moon rises in crimson radiance, throwing a gory splendor over the tableau. I'll stake any Saturday night's receipts against a penny whistle that we send the people home raving.

PROF. Well then, Mr. Snap, I'll tell you the truth about the play. It's not by a friend. It's by myself.

SNAP. I knew it. I knew it from the first. Ah, you can't deceive me, Professor.

PROF. And you will admit that in my position as a leading functionary of the University, and with my family connections opposed to theatrical representations — I can't think of producing the play.

SNAP. Why not ? Your name needn't appear. We announce it — by a gentleman of this city.

PROF. No; it would be sure to leak out. The actors would tell.

SNAP (R.). Rely on us. There's no blabbing in my establishment. My wife sees to that.

PROF. (*crosses to* R.). Your wife ? (*Aside.*) **That re-**

minds me of my wife. If she should discover! (*Aloud.*) No, no. Put it out of your head, Mr. Snap. It won't do.

SNAP (*entreatingly*). And, Professor, don't rob a poor manager of his one chance of making a fortune! (*Keenly.*) And don't rob yourself! Think of the money pouring in when it's brought out in every city of the Union. Your five hundred a week coming in as regularly as your Saturday breakfast.

PROF. (*wavering*). But if it doesn't succeed —

SNAP. Let us put it in rehearsal, and if you say at the last moment, "Don't do it," I'll take it off.

PROF. Well, if you leave that road open for retreat (*impressively*), and pledge the profoundest secrecy

> [SNAP *lays his hand on his heart, and lifts the other heavenward, moving his lips in dumb oath.*

so that I won't run any risk, I may — I say I may make up my mind to consent.

SNAP (*joyfully*). Your mind is made up, Professor! I see it shining on the very tip of your nose.

> [PROFESSOR *touches his nose absently.*

It's settled. (*Wrings his hand.*) I'll bill it for the opening. (*Goes for his coat.*)

PROF. (R.). That's only a week.

SNAP. March 1st! No postponement!

PROF. (*aside*). My wife won't be home for a fortnight at least. That will do very well. (*Aloud.*) Are you sure you can cast all the parts in your troupe?

SNAP. We have cast Shakespeare from end to end. Let me tell you what I'll do for you, Professor. (*Puts MSS. in his coat pocket.*) To prevent any chance of failure, I will play King Titus Tatius myself. I felt that part as I read it.

PROF. (*reflectively*). Yes — but —. He ought to be a person of very large and venerable and imposing presence. Don't you think so?

SNAP. That isn't all, Professor. (*Crosses to* R.   *th an air.*) Grace, royal action, dignity, that's what the part needs. My wife will play Virgia, the heroine. That woman was born for the part — it's written all over her, so to speak.

PROF. Indeed!

SNAP. I've got some of her photos with me. (*Takes photographs from pocket of his ulster, which he has thrown over back of chair,* C.) There she is as Lady Macbeth! (*Hands one to the* PROFESSOR.) There she is as Frou-Frou. There she is as Juliet, and here she is as Olivette. Her range is wonderful.

PROF. It must be.

SNAP. If you'll allow me. (*Takes them back from the* PRO-FESSOR.) I'll leave one here as a memento. I think the Olivette is the best. Gives the best expression — shows more of her. (*Sets photograph of an opéra-bouffe character on table* L., *facing the audience.*) And now, sir, I'll take my leave. (*Puts MSS. in pocket.*)

PROF. (R.). But one word, Mr. Snap. The — the part of Virgia is a — a — a very young girl, and your wife, eh! don't you think?   [*READY* SUSAN, *to enter* L. C.

SNAP. Oh, that doesn't matter! That woman has a power of facial transformation that has paralyzed the critics of two hemispheres. They call her "The Chameleon." Besides, she's the only woman in the company that can play the part. I can see her at this moment at the end of act second, as she flings herself before King Romulus, tears the tunic from her shoulders (*he has his coat half on, and now tears it off, suiting action to word*), casts it at his feet, and cries : —

> " Though keen thy sword ; victorious thy banner,
> Thou canst of life deprive me, not of honor."

(*Drops on his knee, then picks up his coat, etc.*) I have the honor. (*EXITS,* L. C.)

PROF. (*comes forward, rubbing his hands in ecstasy*). If my wife only gives me two weeks longer, and nobody suspects, I'll do it.

SUSAN *ENTERS, hurrying in,* L. C.

SUSAN. Professor, Professor, he's taking our tragedy with him!

PROF. Who?

SUSAN. The manager. I saw it; he had it under his arm.

PROF. (*crossing to* L.). But I tell you —

SUSAN (*slyly*). Ah, Professor! Can't I see how the land lies? It's going to be produced at a real theatre, by real actors.

PROF. (L.). Hush! Don't bellow it all over the place.

SUSAN (*whispers*). Mustn't nobody know it?

PROF. Of course not! Don't you dare to breathe a word of it to anybody — above all, not to my wife. (*Aside.*) I'll write her at once to stay another fortnight. (*Sits at table,* L., *to write.*)

[*READY* MRS. BABBITT, *with satchels and hand-baggage, to enter* L. C.

SUSAN (*while he writes*). Oh, trust me, there sha'n't a soul know of it, not if they was to tear it from me with wild horses. I only thought of it yesterday, Professor, while I was beating the rugs, how, when Missus Babbitt comes home, all our fine times will be over. I'll never forget 'em, Professor (*with emotion*). You a-sitting there evenings a-reading, and a-reading, and the big tears chassaying down my cheeks. And then I'd dream all night I was a-acting every part of it, all by myself, on top of the stage. (*Gesticulates violently, as if acting.*)

PROF. (*looks up from writing, but not heeding her*). If I could only think of a pretext to keep my wife away. Ah, I have it! (SUSAN *drops violently on her knees.* PROFESSOR *writes.*)

[*READY* NISBE, *with flowers, satchels, etc., to enter*
L. C.

SUSAN (*rises*).   One thing is certain ; when the piece is
acted at our theatre, I must be there.   If Mrs. Babbitt won't
let me, I'll run off without leave, and if she packs me off the
next day, I'll console myself with those beautiful lines out of
our play : —

> " And though thy anger have no end,
> Then break my heart ; it shall not bend."

PROF. (*gives her a postal card*).   Mail this postal card at
once.   Egad, Susan, I think I'll put on my coat, and steal
over to the theatre, and have a look at the stage.   (*EXIT,*
L. D.)

SUSAN (*reading from the postal card*).   " My darling : —
I'm sitting all alone at my writing-table, with my solitary cup
of tea."   O Professor !   (*Looks towards* L.)

During the above, MRS. BABBITT *has ENTERED,* L. C., *in
travelling-costume, with satchels and hand-baggage.*

MRS. BABBITT.   Susan, what are you doing there ?

SUSAN (*aside*).   Mercy on us !   Mrs. Babbitt, I declare !

MRS. B. (L.).   What are you reading there ?

SUSAN (*hesitatingly*).   Only a postal card from the Professor to you, ma'am.

MRS. B. (*snatches card*).   And you read it !   Go help Sophonisba with her things.

SUSAN.   Yes 'em.   (*Aside, crossing up* C.)   What will the
Professor do now ?   (*Aloud.*)   Let me help you, Miss Nisbe.

NISBE *ENTERS, loaded up with flowers, satchels, etc.,* L. C.

NISBE (*down* C.).   Never mind me.   Where's papa ?

SUSAN.   The Professor, Miss, he's only in his room, he
was just going to the Opera House.

MRS. B.   To the what ?

SUSAN (L.).   Yes 'em, about the — (*remembers*).   Oh, cricky! (*Aloud.*) For his soda water, ma'am.   He goes there every day for his soda water.

[NISBE *puts her things down.*

MRS. B.   Indeed!   Go and help to bring up our trunks.

SUSAN.   Yes, ma'am.   (*Aside; going.*) Oh, dear, our jig's up now!

NIS. (*going,* L.).   I'll go and tell papa we've come.

MRS. B.   Stay where you are.   We'll surprise him here.

NIS.   How delighted he'll be.   Just after writing to you, too.   What does he say, ma?

MRS. B. (*puts on her glasses and reads*).   "My darling :" — Ah, he always calls me his darling.   "I am sitting alone at my writing-table, with my solitary cup of tea." (*Stops and looks at* NISBE.)

[NISBE *looks at her mother, and then towards the tables,* R. *and* L.

"The household sleeps.   All is silence and darkness, for midnight has just sounded."

NIS.   Midnight!   Why, mamma, it's only quarter to five now.

MRS. B.   There's something strange about this.   (*Reads.*) "Before me on my table stands your portrait."

NIS. (*goes to table and finds the photo which* SNAP *left there. She looks at it and starts*).   O papa!   (*Hastily conceals it.*)

MRS. B.   What's the matter?

[*READY* PROFESSOR, *to enter* L. D.

NIS. (*innocently*).   Oh, nothing.

MRS. B. (*reads*).   "The flowers plucked by my sweet child are in a glass of water before me."

NIS. (*indignant*).   O mamma, they're in the waste-basket!

[*They look at each other, turn away and look round the room.*

MRS. B.   Nothing but falsehoods!   (*Reads.*) "I long to see both of you again; yet, for your own dear sakes, I beg you to remain where you are for another fortnight. Besides, we are quite upside down at home. Susan has just left us " —

Nis.   What?

Mrs. B. (*reads quickly*).   "Poor Susan has flown to the assistance of her aunt in New Haven, who has been seized with a cerebral meningitis. I gave her leave for a week, and she started last night with a few things in my handbag."

Nis.   Mamma! (*Clasping her hands.*)

Mrs. B.   Horrible! (*Sinks in chair.*)

PROFESSOR, L. D., *is heard singing outside.*

Prof.   Then to-night we'll merry, merry be! (*ENTERS and sees them; he has his hat cocked jauntily.*)   Heavens! my wife! (*With exaggerated kindness.*)   Why, my darling Zippy (*crosses to* c.), and dear little Nisbe! — What a glorious surprise! I've so longed for you. Just sent off a postal card begging you to come back as soon as possible. (*Aside.*) I'll write another to-night. (*Crosses to* L.)

Mrs. B. (*rises majestically*).   Professor Babbitt, I have just read the postal card you sent. (*Shows it.*)

Prof. (*aside*).   I'm dished. (*Aloud.*)   Would you believe, my love —

Mrs. B.   I believe nothing. But this I tell you, I've gone to the Springs for the last time. I'll get all the white sulphur I want at home, and so will you.

Prof.   Now, Zippy!

Mrs. B.   Don't touch me. (*EXITS,* R. D.)

[*READY curtain.*

Prof.   Nisbe!

Nis.   And mamma hasn't seen the worst yet! (*Shows him the photo.*)   Is that mamma's portrait?

Prof.   Ye gods! Olivette! (*He sinks in chair.*)

[*She holds picture before him and shakes her finger.*

CURTAIN FALLS.

ACT II.

SCENE. — *Reception room at* DAMASK'S. *A very handsome writing-table,* C., *with desk-chair in front, and an easy-chair near by at* L. *Sofa,* R., *and chair,* L. *Doors,* R. *and* L. *Window,* R. C.

TIME. — *The following afternoon.*

> DAMASK, *in handsome house-jacket and cap, is discovered at desk, writing. He finishes, rings bell, folds paper.* MARIA *ENTERS at* C. *READY* JACK, *to enter* C. *from* L.

DAMASK (*giving her the paper*). Take that to Mrs. Dedalive's as quick as you can. It's a prescription. Tell her she'll find full directions inside. (MARIA *takes letter and EXITS,* C. *and* L.) I'm afraid my wife needs a prescription more than anybody. She went to bed with a headache last night, had breakfast sent up to her this morning, kept her room at lunch-time, and has been speechless, to me, all the while. And all because I have no past. Was anything ever so ridiculous! It's a bad case. I really believe I must have a consultation over it.

> MARIA, C. *from* L., *ENTERS with her hat and shawl on, and with a card on a tray.*

MARIA. A gentleman called just as I was going out, sir.
DAM. (R., *reads*). "Alfred Chumley, with Snap's Dramatic Combination." (*Shakes his head.*) Don't know him.
MAR. If you please, sir, he wrote something on the other side.

DAM. Oh, did he? (*Turns card and reads.*) " Behind the unsuggestive alias of Chumley is concealed the identity of your old college chum — Jack Mulberry." (*Speaks delightedly.*) Jack Mulberry! (*To* MARIA.) Show him in at once. (*She EXITS. He reads.*) " Who, remembering the pleasant days we spent together as students at Leipzig, asks your friendly aid in a matter of importance."

JACK *ENTERS*, C. *from* L.

JACK (L. C.). Old fellow!

DAM. (R.). Jack, old boy! Is it possible you are an actor, and in America? [*Shake hands ; then they embrace.*

JACK. Transformation, isn't it? The idle drone in the hive of learning turned industrious worker in the flowery garden of the drama. Behold me! Leading juvenile, eccentric comedian, light, very light tenor in comic opera, with Snap's Central Park Dramatic Menagerie!

DAM. But, my dear boy, with your family, your prospects! What brought you to it?

JACK. The path that leads to all folly! (*Crosses to* R.). The thorny path of love and recklessness. You recollect, I was always in love.

DAM. I remember our Hebrew professor's daughter.

JACK. We exchanged sighs, glances, smiles, letters, and vows of love for several months.

DAM. (L.). You had got as far as that when I left the University.

JACK. And I stopped there. It appears I was only tenant at will of her heart — subject to a month's notice to quit. I was ejected. Our Greek tutor moved in with a lease for life ; that is, she married him.

DAM. So far all's well.

JACK. Worse remains behind. I went home, completed my education in London with a finishing course of fast life, and ended by falling at the feet of a charming little serio comic singer at the Canterbury.

DAM. (*impatiently*).   You idle fellows are all of a piece. I really am not surprised now at my wife.   She takes us to be all alike.   How did you get out of this scrape?

JACK.   I didn't get out of it.   That's what I'm here for. You can help me.

DAM.   Excuse me !   (*Crosses to* R.)   I decline to interfere in these irregularities.

JACK.   My dear old Socrates, you misunderstand.   The irregularity is all over.

DAM.   You are sure ?

JACK.   Turned over a new leaf.   Spanked Cupid, and turned him out of my house.   Closed the books, made up my accounts, and am ready to submit them to your inspection with the proper vouchers.   Will you listen ?

DAM.   Certainly.   [*Both sit.*

JACK (*pulls a Russia leather pocket-book from his pocket*). To begin.   The little queen of Canterbury was a charming creature.   The proof of the fact is contained in Exhibit A — her portrait.

DAM. (*takes it*).   Extremely pretty.

JACK.   Eyes of heavenly blue.   Tresses of raven blackness.   Exhibit B — tress cf raven blackness !   (*Hands over a small black curl, tied with pink ribbon.*)

DAM. (*takes it*).   Well?

JACK.   We became acquainted on a beautiful summer evening ; and as a proof of her maidenly attachment, she presented me with a rose.   Exhibit C — remains of rose. (*Hands over a crushed rosebud.*)

DAM.   Very appropriate.   (*Takes it.*)

JACK.   When we pledged our undying attachment, she gave me, in eternal remembrance, a little ring of twisted gold.   Exhibit D.   (*Takes out ring and polishes it on his sleeve.*)   Looks like gold, doesn't it?

DAM.   The whole thing suggests unmitigated brass.

JACK.   So far all is mere trifling.   What oppresses me most is Exhibit E.   (*Draws from his book a package of bills.*) Take them.   (*Turns away as he hands them over, and puts his hand to his eyes.*)

DAM.   Unpaid?   (*Looks over the package.*)

JACK.   Mostly.   They were the cause of our separation. The governor refused to send me any more money.   It affected her so deeply that she wrote to me that we must part; that she was resolved to bury herself from the world. I subsequently learned that she had dyed Exhibit B (*takes up curl*) as yellow as Exhibit D (*shows ring*) and was playing Boccaccio in Dublin.   (*Rises; crosses to* R.)

DAM.   In Dublin?   That was hard.   And you drove her to it?   [*READY* ANGELICA, *to enter* R.

JACK.   You can imagine the rest.   Remorse drove me to New York.   I pawned my gold watch — stop a minute! Here's the ticket.   Exhibit F — pawn-ticket for watch. (*Shows it, then replaces it and the rest of the articles in the pocket-book, which he hands to* DAMASK.)   And then I went on the stage.   I hadn't a particle of talent for it, of course, but I joined a bread-and-butter company, and go through the country for my board — when I can get it.   (*Crosses to* L.) But now I'm sick and tired of the whole business.   I wish to go home like the Prodigal and ask my good-hearted dad for pardon.   So far he has sent back my letters unopened. But he thinks the world of you, for you were the best and soberest of all my college friends.   So if you will only write to him —

DAM.   (*taking his hand*).   Certainly.   I'll do it at once. I'll send him all these documents with a strong personal letter, and if you will add a few lines of contrition at the end, you'll be sure of forgiveness.   (*Puts the articles in pocket-book, and locks it up in his desk.*)   [*Both rise.*

JACK.   I saw by the morning paper that my governor has

Just arrived in New York, so we'll set about it to-day. I'll get the name of his hotel, and you can write at once to him.

DAM. To-day.

ANGELICA *ENTERS at* R.

My dear, I'm delighted to see you down. Allow me — (*introducing*) an old friend of my college days; you've often heard me speak of Jack Mulberry.

JACK. Quite so! Charmed, I'm sure.

ANGELICA (*crosses to* C., *politely*). An old friend of my husband's, and from such a distance! (*Gives her hand.*) Quite interesting. (*Aside.*) His chum at college. (*To* DAM-ASK.) My love — (*with a sweet smile*).

DAM. (R.). Yes, dear.

ANG. I left my *Century* on the table in my room; won't you send it to mamma for me?

DAM. Certainly, my love. (*To* JACK.) See you in a few moments, Jack. (*EXIT*, R.)

ANG. (*aside*). He shall give me the facts about my gentleman's past. (*Aloud.*) You must consider our house your own while you stay here, Mr. Mulberry My husband will want to talk over old times with you. (*Sits on sofa*, R.)

JACK. Oh, I shall be delighted — but —

ANG. (*not heeding*). Oh, he has told me all about them. Such stories! Such adventures — well, according to his own account, he was the wildest among you.

JACK (*aside*). Harry's been romancing to the confiding soul.

ANG. I suppose he led you off now and then?

JACK. Well — yes; that is, now and then. Yes, when he didn't go it too strong.

ANG. Oh, I always love to hear him tell about it. Then he didn't exaggerate when he told me he was dubbed "the heart-breaker."

JACK (*aside*). Heart-breaker! Poor Harry. Meek as a

mouse. If she's so proud of it, I suppose I'd better humor the fancy.

ANG. You don't answer.

JACK (L., *of table*). Oh, he was right. His adventures would fill volumes.   [*READY* DAMASK, *to re-enter* R.

ANG. (*rises; aside, in agony*). Oh, heavens! (*Aloud.*) Really? I'm so glad. I thank you very much for your information. (*Gives her hand and turns away.*)

JACK (*aside*). Something's wrong here. I think I'd better go before I commit Harry further. (*Aloud.*) If you will permit me — a very pressing engagement. (*Gets his hat.*)

ANG. Must you?

JACK. I must. There's no telling what might be the consequences if I didn't. (*Aside.*) She looks like Cassandra! (*Aloud.*) Say to Harry that I'll run in again presently.

ANG. (*aside*). He did have a past, after all! (*She is looking away from him and intently at door,* R.)

JACK. Eh? Oh! (*Aside.*) The lady seems to be holding an animated conversation with herself. (*Aloud.*) Just say to Harry!—Eh?—Yes, exactly!—Ahem! Good-morning! (*EXITS hurriedly,* C. *and* L.)

ANG. (*to and fro with an outburst*). It is true, then! Now he must confess, confess all!

DAMASK *RE-ENTERS,* R.

DAM. (R.). Here's the magazine, dear, but Maria went out for me and hasn't got back yet. (*Looks around.*) Where's Jack?

ANG. (*sternly*). Never mind Jack.

DAM. (*looks at her*). What's the matter? Because I didn't send the maga—

ANG. Never mind the magazine. Couldn't you see it was a pretext to get rid of you while I questioned your friend about your past life? (*Crosses to* R.)

DAM. (*stares at her, and then slams the magazine down in a pet*). Well, of all the insanities!

ANG. Hush, sir! You would tell me nothing. I had to apply to him.

DAM. (*mildly*). My dear, this is monomania. You are getting in a very bad way. I thought at first you were only joking, but now —! (*Flings himself into chair.*)

ANG. At first I was only joking, but I thought it over and over last night, and this morning it has become a sad conviction. (*Goes to him and puts her hand on his shoulder lovingly.*) If you would only understand me. I am not so childish as to be jealous of your past.

[*He moves chair round so as to face her, and regards her with a puzzled look.*

But I love you too much to be satisfied with the part some women assume towards their husbands' inner self.

[*He rises.*

(*She places her arms around his neck.*) I wish to be your friend, your confidante! And it is therefore my right to know every secret of your heart! (*Sobbing.*) I — I — never conceal anything from you.

DAM. (*takes her hands from his neck and holds them*). But if I haven't any secrets?

ANG. (*emotionally*). Harry! Open your heart to me.

DAM. I would willingly — if I could.

ANG. O Harry, do it! [*He impatiently passes her.* I have watched you when you thought you were alone. Have seen you gazing into vacancy

[*He turns away his head to conceal his amusement.* as if some dark memory oppressed you. Just as you look now. [*He shakes with silent laughter.* You are moved; I see, I feel it. Oh, it is impossible that the life of a man like you should never have been stirred by the upheaval of some volcanic passion. Tell me, tell me, — please do. (*Falls on his neck.*)

DAM. (*turns his face to her with affected solemnity*). Will you promise, solemnly promise, never to revert to the topic again, if I comply with your wish?

ANG. I promise solemnly.

DAM. On that condition I will tell you — the story. (*Crosses to* L.)

ANG. (*breathless*). Yes, yes!

DAM. (*looks at her*). And you will forgive me everything?

ANG. Everything.

DAM. Well, then! (*He goes to his desk*, C., *and unlocks his drawer. She sinks into chair near by, riveted. He takes out* JACK'S *pocket-book*.) Listen.

ANG. (*aside*). At last!

DAM. (*after a moment's pause, and holding the pocket-book in his hand*). While I was a student at Leipzig, I ran on now and then to Paris, and plunged into the gayeties of the capital. I was a constant attendant at the *cafés chantants* in the Champs–Élysées.

ANG. (*delighted*). Now you see, you never told me that before. (*Jumps up and kisses him.*) Oh, you darling! (*Sits* L. *of table.*)

DAM. I made the acquaintance of one of the most distinguished prima donnas of the period. Here is the picture. (*Takes photo out of the book and hands it to her.*)

ANG. (*looks at it, sets her lips firmly, stiffens up, sighs, shakes her head, and then in low tone*). And you loved her?

DAM. To distraction! She gave me a rose. This one! (*Hands it over.* ANGELICA *lets her hands fall in her lap contemplatively.*) And when I passionately asked her for greater proofs of affection, she cut off a tress of her silken hair. Take it!

ANG. (*takes it; eyes it critically, holding it up daintily*). Well?

DAM. Yes, there is more to come. In the intoxication

of my wild infatuation, I gave her a gold ring (ANGELICA *starts*); but I got it back again. Here it is.

ANG. (*taking it*). Of course you smothered her with presents?

DAM. Oh, awfully!

[*READY* NISBE *and* MRS. BABBITT, *to enter* C. *from* L.

ANG. And ran madly into debt?

DAM. Unfortunately! Here are the bills. (*Gives them.*) Mostly unpaid. Finally I pawned my grandfather's watch. Here's the ticket. (*Gives it and rises.*) And now you know all!

ANG. (*rises, reflectively*). And this happened (*counts on her fingers*) five years ago. Does it worry you now? (*Puts all the things back into pocket-book and lays book on table.*)

DAM. (*sighs*). It does oppress me. But gone is gone.

ANG. (*comes to him*). And the sequel? (*Lays her head on his shoulder.*)

DAM. Haven't you got enough?

ANG. What became of her?

DAM. Poor girl! She took the veil. (*Crosses to* L.)

ANG. And her relatives; had she nobody?

DAM. (*puzzled, scratches his head*). Oh, yes. An uncle.

ANG. (R., *stepping back a step*). He called you to account! He challenged you!

DAM. Oh, yes; he gave me no end of trouble. He was bloodthirsty to a degree.

ANG. And you have borne all this in silence so long! Harry, I love you! (*Throws her arms about him.*) I worship you!

NISBE *ENTERS* C., *from* L., *sees the picture, laughs and calls off.*

NISBE. Mamma! Hurry! A picture of domestic bliss.

MRS. BABBITT *ENTERS* C., *from* L.

MRS. BABBITT (L.). What is it?

DAM. (*aside to* ANGELICA, *as she starts away*). Don't tell your mother a word of all this.

ANG. Never! (*Goes to* MRS. BABBITT *as* DAMASK *greets* NISBE.) O mamma, I'm so delighted to see you! (*Draws her down and impressively, aside.*) Come to my room! I've something most important to tell you.

MRS. B. (*same*). Very well! (*They separate.*)

DAM. (*crosses to* MRS. BABBITT). Well, mamma? Was I not right to advise the Springs? You look ten years younger.

MRS. B. (L.) You're more of a flatterer than a physician, I'm afraid. I'm not at all well.

DAM. Dear me! (*Talks with her.*)

ANG. (*up* R. C. *to* NISBE). Keep Harry here, while I take mamma to my room.

NIS. I understand. (*Takes off her hat, etc.*)

MRS. B. (*crosses to* L. C., *up stage*). Angelica, how's your parrot?

ANG. He's in my room. He's learned ever so many words since you were here last.

DAM. Yes; picked them up from us! He says "kiss me, darling," all day long. He got that from Angelica.

NIS. Oh, I must hear him say that!

ANG. (*aside to her*). Stay where you are! (*Aloud.*) Come, mamma.

NIS. (*crosses to* DAMASK). I want to hear him say "kiss me, darling."

DAM. (*crosses to* R. C., *darting to door*). I'll fetch him.

ANG. (*takes up pocket-book from table*, C.). What for? We can go to him just as well. (*Motions to* NISBE.) Come, mamma. (R., *EXITS quickly, with* MRS. BABBITT.)

DAM. We'll all go!   [NISBE *detains him.*

NIS. O Harry! I want to ask you something. (*He turns at the door. She goes to him.*)

DAM. Not just yet! (*Aside.*) I think I hear them going over Exhibit A now!

NIS. (L., *linking his arm*). Yes, yes. It's very important.

DAM. Do be quick as possible, then. (*Glares off*, R.)

NIS. (*brings him down*). Since our return from the Springs, I've had several strange attacks.

DAM. Yes, yes; all right. (*Aside, looking* R.) She's telling her mother everything.

NIS. (*lets go his arm*). You're not listening!

DAM. Yes, I am; go on!

NIS. (*extending her arm*). Feel my pulse. Don't you notice anything?

DAM. (*looking off* R., *and grasping her thumb by mistake*). No.

NIS. (*draws thumb away indignantly*). After I get up in the morning and have my breakfast — (*gulps*).

DAM. Well, what then?

NIS. *Then* there's nothing. But after breakfast I go out for a walk for about half an hour.

DAM. Well, if walking for half an hour doesn't agree with you, stay at home for half an hour.

NIS. But it does agree with me.

[*READY* JACK, *with note, to enter* C. *from* L.

DAM. All right, go then. (*Going.*)

NIS. (*holding him back*). But something strange happened in my walk this morning. I saw some roses —

DAM. (*aside*). Roses! Exhibit C. (*Aloud.*) Let me go. I must see Angelica.

NIS. (*holds him*). Near the roses stood a young man! (DAMASK *turns and looks at her.*) I didn't take any notice of him (*gulps*); but at the mere sight of the roses, I suddenly grew dizzy, my heart began to palpitate, everything grew black, as if I were going to faint. (*Sinks into chair.*)

DAM. Faint! I'll get you something! (*Darts off*, R. D.)

NIS. No, no; stay here! It's coming over me again. Oh! Oh! (*Sinks in chair, pretending to faint. Short pause. Looks up cautiously and, finding herself alone, bounds up.*)

He got away after all! Well, I did the best I could for Angy. The heartless monster, to leave me in a fainting condition.   [JACK *coughs outside.*
(*Listens.*) No, he's coming back. Now I'll give him a swoon as is a swoon. (*Throws herself in a chair, closes her eyes and groans.*) ·Oh! Oh! Oh!

JACK *ENTERS* c. *from* L., *with a note.*

JACK. I've jotted down a few more points for Harry, in writing his letter. (*Sees* NISBE.) What's that? A young lady! Seems to be ill.

NIS. (*her eyes still closed, rolls her head languidly*). Oh! Oh!

JACK (*looks around*). If I could find the cologne. (*Sees an atomizer on the table.*) Here's something. (*Takes it up and squeezes the cologne over her face.*)

NIS. (*groans feebly, with her eyes still closed.*) Oh, how refreshing! Do it some more.

JACK (*aside*). By Jove! she's pretty. (*Repeats bus.*)

NIS. (*same*). Bathe my forehead.

JACK (R., *looks around*). Where is the water? (*Not finding it, resumes the atomizer.*)

NIS. That's it. Now a little back of my ear!
                                                [JACK *obeys.*
Oh, how reviving!

JACK (*aloud, suddenly*). Do you feel better now?

NIS. (*opens her eyes suddenly, then starts up*). A stranger! Heavens!

JACK. Pardon me, if I startled you; but I thought it my duty to come to your assistance.

NIS. I'm so much obliged! But I — I — I thought it was my brother-in-law.

JACK. I am too happy in having arrived at the right moment, especially as my medical knowledge — (*unconsciously squeezes the atomizer, and gets the cologne in his eyes*).

NIS. (L.). Are you a doctor, too?

JACK. Not exactly. But I studied medicine for one term with my friend Harry. My name is Jack Mulberry.

NIS. Dr. Damask is my brother-in-law.

JACK. Then I have the pleasure of addressing the Professor's daughter.

NIS. (*quickly*). Yes; but don't tell papa of my fainting, please.

JACK. I wouldn't dream of it for the world. Besides, I perceived at once you were merely practising a little deception on somebody.

NIS. (*severely*). Practising a deception?

JACK. Of course. You recovered too suddenly.

NIS. Allow me — it was very serious. I have these attacks repeatedly. (*Crosses to* R.)

JACK (*aside*). The little fibber!

NIS. If you understand anything about medicine, you must perceive that I have a fever. Be kind enough to feel my pulse. (*She holds out her hand, the thumb uppermost. As* JACK *advances to feel her pulse, she turns her thumb down.*)

JACK. Certainly, a very strong fever! (*Aside.*) Not a trace.

NIS. (*triumphantly*). There now!

JACK. I offer my humblest apologies. I begin to see your case clearly. Before these attacks come on you have a buzzing in your ears? [*She nods.*

A mist comes over your eyes? [*She nods.*

Hammering in your head? [*Same bus.*

Twitching sensation in your hands? [*Same bus.*

One foot cold as ice, the other burning hot?

NIS. (R.). Yes, yes. What do you advise?

JACK. You wish to know?

NIS. Yes; I'm prepared for anything.

JACK. Well, then, I advise you to invent some other illness.

NIS. (*indignantly*). What?

JACK. Or devote more care to the statement of your symptoms.

NIS. Do you mean to —

JACK. I mean to say that the condition you described never existed, except in the imagination.

NIS. You should have taken another course of lessons, Doctor. (*Crosses to* L.) You never got as far as my complaint. (*Very sarcastically.*)

JACK (*cheerfully*). Possibly, possibly. And I never regretted so much as now that I rejected science to go on the stage.

NIS. Are you an actor?

JACK. Well, some people think I'm not. Fact is, I merely imagined I could be one. Having discovered my mistake, I give it up cheerfully. My last appearance will be as Cassius, a young Roman, in your father's tragedy.

NIS. Father's tragedy! Papa has written a tragedy?

JACK (*aside*). She doesn't know it. How awkward of me!

NIS. And it's going to be produced?

JACK. I ought not to have mentioned it.

NIS. Oh, yes, you ought, and you must tell me all about it. I'm burning to know.

JACK. No, no! We are pledged to secrecy, and it slipped out. (*Mutters to himself, aside.*)

NIS. (*aside*). More mystery about papa. That accounts for the portrait and the soda water at the Opera House.

JACK. Now I think of it, the piece is not by your father, but by some other professor's daughter's father. I got the names confused.

NIS. (*aside*). I do believe he can fib like a girl. We'll see. (*Aloud.*) Oh, yes; I know what you mean now. It's that old tragedy they found in the college library. (*Eyes him keenly.*)

JACK. Oh, yes; found in an old chest in the cellar. Yes, t's the very one.

NIS.   The plot is all about the persecutions of the early Christians, under Numa Pompilius.

[*READY* PROFESSOR, *to enter* C. *from* L.

JACK.   You've got it; I play Cassius.   I'm an early Christian; they persecute me.   But don't tell your papa.   Promise me.

NIS.   No, I won't.   But you must promise me something, too.

JACK.   With pleasure.   What?

NIS.   Invent some other plot for your next tragedy.

JACK.   What?

NIS.   Or pay more attention to your historical dates.   Just imagine!   Persecutions of the Christians under Numa Pompilius!   Why he died seven hundred years before the Christian Era!   (*Crosses to* R.)

JACK.   Horrible!   I forgot I was talking to a professor's daughter.   I apologize again.   Seems to me, I'm always apologizing.

NIS.   Don't worry.   We're quits now for my fainting spell.

JACK.   And I'm forgiven?

NIS.   Fully.

JACK.   Oh, thanks!   (*He is about to take her hand when*)

The PROFESSOR *ENTERS*, C. *from* L.

The author of her being and of the play!

PROFESSOR (*aside*).   Our leading juvenile!   (*Aloud.*) What are you doing here?

JACK.   I — I — have a letter for Dr. Damask.

PROF.   Indeed!   (*Suspiciously.*)   I wonder if these fellows make love off the stage as well as they do on it?

NIS.   (R. *with composure*).   My brother-in-law is in the next room.

JACK.   Is he?   Well, then, I'll take my leave.   (*Bows, going, aside.*)   She's lovely and she's clever!   My first encounter with one of the institutions of the country — an

American girl! I hope I'll see more of it. (*EXITS*, c. and l.)

NIS. (R., *brings* PROFESSOR *down*). Papa, I think it's very unfair to have secrets from me!

PROF.   What secrets?

NIS.   You know I always stand by you.

PROF. (*softens*).   Well, then?

NIS. (*mysteriously*).   I know all! You have written a tragedy.

PROF.   For goodness' sake, not so loud. (*Crosses to* R.) If your mother should hear! (*Piteously.*) Only think, she hasn't spoken a kind word to me since she got back from the Springs.

NIS. (*solemnly*).   How did we find you when we did get back?

PROF.   Has she spoken to you about it?

NIS.   Not a syllable.

PROF.   She's a dreadfully uncomfortable woman. She keeps things for days, leaves you in an awful state of apprehension, and then springs at you when you least expect it. Do me one favor.   Don't leave me alone with her any more than you possibly can.

      [*READY* MRS. BABBITT, *with pocket-book, etc., to*
        enter R. D.

NIS. (*in thought*).   Papa, is Cassius a nice part?

PROF.   Cassius? Oh! (*Brightening.*) Of course he is. He's the hero.   Has a magnificent love scene in the second act.   Stabs himself in the third.

NIS.   Doesn't he come in after the third act?

PROF.   How can he, after stabbing himself? (*Crosses to* L.)

NIS. (R.).   I think the interest will flag then. It's a great pity.

PROF.   No, it won't. (*Rubs his hands.*) I saw the rehearsal this morning.

NIS.   How did you like it?

PROF. I don't know. I was so excited, it seemed like a dream.

NIS. Aren't you awfully nervous?

PROF. I didn't sleep a wink last night.

NIS. Tell me, papa, whom does Cassius make love to?

MRS. BABBITT *ENTERS*, R. D., *carrying the pocket-book and bills in her hand. The* PROFESSOR *avoids her.*

PROF. Sh! Here's your mother.

MRS. B. Nisbe! (*Icy tones as she sees the* PROFESSOR.) Oh! you're there?

PROF. (*crosses, yet avoiding her eye*). Yes, my love; you see I couldn't deny myself the pleasure of calling for you.

MRS. B. Indeed! Nisbe, go to your sister. She wants you.

NIS. (*crosses to the* PROFESSOR, *who has gesticulated violently—pantomiming her to stay*). O mamma, just as I was having such a nice talk with papa, whom I haven't seen for so long!

PROF. No, we haven't seen each other for so long. (*Continues his motions.*)

MRS. B. (L., *to* NISBE *icily*). I wish to speak with your father alone! (*Sits* L.)

PROF. That settles it. (*Sinks into chair* R. *of table.*) Now for it!

NIS. (*aside*). Poor papa! (*Going, and aside to him.*) Cheer up! (*EXITS*, R. D.)

PROF. (*aside, as* MRS. BABBITT *turns on him*). The juggernaut approaches.

MRS. B. (L.). You are aware, Mr. Babbitt, that you owe me some explanations?

PROF. (*rises, confidently, clearing his throat*). I'm quite ready, my dear.

MRS. B. (*repressing him by an imperious wave of the hand*). You are quite ready with a tissue of inventions, no doubt.

PROF. Now, my darling —

MRS. B. I spare you the trouble. There is something, unfortunately, of graver importance. I must have at least five hundred dollars.

PROF. Five hundred dollars! (*Aghast.*)

MRS. B. At once.

PROF. Will you please explain?

MRS. B. No. I forego explanations from you, and reserve all on my own part. Get me the money; the matter admits of no delay. (*Crosses to* R.)

PROF. But where am I to get it?

MRS. B. Take it out of Nisbe's money.

PROF. (*aside*). And I've just borrowed from Nisbe's money to meet some expenses at the —

[*READY* ANGELICA *and* DAMASK, *to enter* R.

MRS. B. What are you saying?

PROF. (L.). You wouldn't have me touch the child's pittance?

MRS. B. We can save up and replace it in a year. Give me the key of the safe.

PROF. (*aside*). She'll find I've been there already.

MRS. B. Well!

PROF. The fact is, my darling, I've just had to call in her investment, and happen to have the money with me. I just got it from the bank. (*Fumbles in his pocket.*)

MRS. B. All the better. (*Holds out her hand.*)

PROF. (*takes out pocket-book and produces a single bank-bill*). My beautiful fresh greenback! (*Hands it.*)

MRS. B. (*snatching it*). Five hundred dollars all in one bill! (*Examines it.*)

PROF. Yes. You nearly made it in two. That's how it goes so easily. (*Aside.*) My last cent, and to-morrow the first of the month.

ANGELICA *and* DAMASK *ENTER,* R. *He is sulky and keeps his hands in his pockets. She is clinging to one arm sweetly.*

ANG. (*aside to* DAMASK *as they enter*).   Will you see that my telling her was all for the best?

DAM. (L. C.).   Good-morning, Professor!   (*Struck by his dejected air.*)   You don't look well.   Anything the matter?

> [PROFESSOR *stretches out his hand gloomily to shake.* DAMASK *takes hold of his pulse and pulls out his watch to count.* PROFESSOR *snatches his hand away.* DAMASK *shrugs his shoulders and they separate.*

MRS. B. (*draws* ANGELICA *down front and gives her the bank-note and the pocket-book cautiously*).   There are five hundred dollars to pay your husband's sinful debts.

ANG. (*gushingly*).   O mamma!

MRS. B.   No thanks. . Thank goodness, I had it.

ANG.   O mamma, how good you are!   (*Tries to embrace her.*)

MRS. B. (*draws back*).   Hush!   (*Crosses to* PROFESSOR.)   Are you going to be at home this evening, Mr. Babbitt?

PROF. (*injured tone and look*).   Do I ever go out?

MRS. B.   Yes — for soda water.

> [*He retires up stage.   She follows him.*

ANG. (R.   *Beckons* DAMASK *down to her.   Gives him the pocket-book and the bank-bill*).   Now you see how much better it was to confess everything to me.   There are five hundred dollars!   Pay those dreadful debts and close the transaction forever!

DAM. (*surprised and amused*).   What? five hun —

ANG. (*cautiously*).   Hush!   It's a little torn, but —

DAM.   You are an angel!   (*Tries to embrace her.*)

> [*She draws back, her fingers to her lips, and joins her mother.   They hurry off,* R., *in animated conversation.*

ANG.   Come, mamma!   Nisbe's waiting.   (*EXIT with* MRS. BABBITT, R. D.)

DAM. (*looks at bank-note*).   Providence takes care of its

own! (*Pockets money, and locks pocket-book in drawer.*) If it pays as well as this, I'll tell her a few more anecdotes of my past life. (*Sits R. of table.*)

PROF. (*who has walked the stage dolefully, stops and eyes* DAMASK). Shall I try and raise the money from my son-in-law? He never seems to have any surplus change, but here goes. (*Comes down.*) Will you have a cigar, Harry? I just bought some. (*Takes a paper parcel from his pocket, unwraps it, and produces two cigars.*)

DAM. The poor old gentleman's favorite — Key Wests! I couldn't rob you, sir ; smoke one with me. (*Offers cigars from case.*)

PROF. I dare say yours are the best. (*Wraps his own up again, and pockets them. Takes a cigar from* DAMASK, *and gets a match from his pocket as* DAMASK *takes out his match-case.*) No, no; I'll furnish the matches. Fair play, you know.

[*They light.* PROFESSOR *holding the match, burns his fingers. He eyes* DAMASK.

DAM. You don't smoke!

[*READY* SNAP, *to enter* C. *from* L.

PROF. The fact is, Harry, I'm in a little trouble. I want to ask a favor of you.

DAM. Certainly, sir; what is it?

PROF. Could you help me out with a little money for a few months?

DAM. (*smoking*). With pleasure.

PROF. (*delighted*). Really?

DAM. (*feeling in his pocket*). How much?

PROF. It's a very large sum.

DAM. Don't hesitate to name it. Anything in reason. (*Stage,* R.)

PROF. (*gasping*). Five — hundred — dollars!

DAM. (*coolly*). Mere trifle. (*Turns half away, unfolds bank-note, while the* PROFESSOR *looks on excitedly.*) Here you are.

PROF. Harry, you're a noble fellow.

DAM. You don't mind its being in one bill, I suppose? (*Hands it over.*)

PROF. (*crosses to* R.). One bill! (*Opens it. Aside.*) My bill! He swindled it out of my wife, the young robber. (*Pockets it.*) Well, he'll never get that back again.

SNAP *ENTERS, hurriedly, at back. Sees the* PROFESSOR, *and comes forward.*

SNAP. Thank goodness,˙ I've found you at last.! I've come straight from your house. (*Puts down his hat and produces MSS. of the play.*)

PROF. (R., *alarmed*). What do you want here? Go away! (*Points vigorously to* DAMASK.)

DAM. (*smoking*). Ah, Snap! (*To* PROFESSOR.) I hope you're not to back up Snap with my five hundred.

SNAP (*smiling to* DAMASK). How d'ye do, sir? (*To* PROFESSOR.) Oh, I made the doctor's acquaintance this morning. He took two seats for the opening. (*Crossing to* C., *inquiringly, half aside.*) Does he know?

PROF. (*important*). No, he does not.

DAM. (L.). But he'd be glad to. What is it?

[SNAP *puts his finger beside his nose.*

PROF. (*crosses to* C. *To* DAMASK, *hurriedly*). I rely on your discretion. He comes about my play — my tragedy; it's going to be played — in the strictest confidence.

DAM. By Jove! Good! I admire your pluck, dad-in-law.

PROF. (*to* SNAP). Now, what is it? You had no business to come here. My wife may be in at any moment.

SNAP. Oh, if we're caught, we can pass it off with a little presence of mind. Say that I'm an old friend of yours, or a stranger visiting the university.

DAM. I think, on the whole, we'd better not rely on our presence of mind. Your absence of body would be better.

PROF. (*nervously*). But what do you want?

SNAP (*recalled to business*). Oh, just so! (*Opens the*

MSS.)   It's about the part of Tullia, the female slave, you know. We haven't a soul to play it.

PROF. (R.).   No one to play Tullia !   Why, she's one of the principal parts of the piece. She gives it its name. She's the Beautiful Sabine !   What's to be done ?

SNAP.   I've talked it over with my wife. That woman is invaluable for expedients. You couldn't corner that woman if you were Shakespeare himself. She found a way out of the difficulty immediately. Instead of Tullia, a female slave, we make it Tullius, a male slave, and there you are.

PROF.   It's impossible !   (*Crosses to* C.)   I can't make her a male slave. Remember her soliloquy in the first act : " Ah, that I were a — that I were a — man !" You can't have a man speak that.

SNAP (R., *puzzled*).   True !   The subtle significance of the aspiration would be lost.

PROF.   Well, then — ?

SNAP.   Well, then, if we can't make her a man, and we haven't got a woman, there's only one thing left. We make it a child — see ?   " Oh, that I were — that I were a — man !" which he isn't, and there you are.

PROF.   A child !   No, I won't submit to have the part cut down like that.

SNAP.   It'll add to the piece immensely. My youngest boy, Tom, will take the part, and make it the hit of the performance.

PROF.   You really think it would do ?

SNAP.   I should say so. That child of mine is a born genius. Just go over the lines, won't you, and cut out the long words. I've brought the book.

PROF.   You want me to alter all the part on the spot ?

SNAP.   Must. We rehearse again to-night.

PROF.   Then come with me. Harry, keep everybody out of this room. (*EXITS,* L. D., *with MSS.*)

SNAP.   Very good, Professor. (*Sees him off and returns.*)

By the way, Doctor, my wife's heard about your wife's parrot, and she's dying to bring it on in "The Beautiful Sabine."

SNAP. No, no; but the second act is set in a grove of pines, and she thought it would look realistic to have the parrot discovered on one of the pine-trees. Bit of realism — see? These things take immensely.

DAM. (L.). Is there a parrot in the play?

DAM. Have you got a pine-tree?

SNAP. Not exactly a pine-tree, but my wife has hit on a capital substitute. She saw an orange plant in a tub at the drug store, and got the loan of it for the run of the play. We give the druggist a line on the bills for its use. Just fancy, a live parrot on a real orange-tree. The audience would be transported to Rome in an instant.

DAM. Why, old man, you're going to make a regular spectacle of it. How about your costumes? Got a full Roman wardrobe?

SNAP. I should say so. My wife made 'em all for the "La Belle Hélène." (*Crosses to* L., *stops and rubs his ear.*) There was a hitch though at one time. We hadn't anything for the Sabine warriors to wear.

DAM. And how did you manage?

SNAP. My wife did it. When we went to sleep last night, there were all the Sabine warriors before our minds' eye without a rag on. In the middle of the night, just as I was dreaming of the hundredth performance of the piece, she gave a scream that nearly threw me out of bed. "I have it!" she cried; and she had. We are going to have a company of firemen for the Sabine army, you know. Well, we make them wear their red shirts outside, with tights, and there you are.

[*READY* MRS. BABBITT, *to RE-ENTER* R. D.

DAM. (*throws himself into chair, laughing*). Ha! ha! ha! The Sabine army in red shirts!

SNAP. I believe the effect will be striking.

DAM. It will be. I wouldn't miss it for the world Snap, you are the prince of barn-stormers. (*Crosses to* L.)

SNAP. Barn-stormers! Who were the first actors? Barn-stormers. Who was Roscius? A barn-stormer! Or Garrick—or Kean? Barn-stormers! Perhaps I don't always pay my salaries, and can't always take my trunks away— but all the more glory for getting on in spite of it. Where's your school for genius? We have it! Who in his time plays many parts? We do! Barn-stormers, indeed! Barn-stormers!! (*EXITS, in high indignation, after the* PRO-FESSOR.)

DAM. Bravo, Snap! I like a man to stand up for his trade.

MRS. BABBITT *RE–ENTERS*, R. D.

MRS. B. You seem in remarkably good spirits. (DAM-ASK *instantly becomes grave. She looks around.*) I thought I heard high words.

DAM. You didn't expect to hear low language, I hope.

MRS. B. This is no time for trifling, Henry. My daughter has told me everything.

DAM. In spite of my express injunctions!

MRS. B. It was her duty, as my child.

DAM. And what was her duty, as my wife?

MRS. B. How can you talk of duty after the revelations you have made?

DAM. (*aside*). I'm afraid we've made a nice mess, after all.

MRS. B. You perceive that I do not use violent re-proaches. I will even shield you. Angelica's father shall know nothing.

DAM. That being the case, let's say no more about it.

MRS. B. It's a subject that will not bear discussion; I shall simply act. (*He looks at her.*) I will take the settlement of this affair into my own hands.

DAM. I don't quite comprehend.

MRS. B. I doubt if there is another mother-in-law who would act with so much dignity and tact.

DAM. (R.). No; it's remarkable.

MRS. B. (L.). I only require from you the whole truth. First of all, about that unfortunate girl. Is everything over between you?

DAM. (*solemnly*). Forever!

MRS. B. That is satisfactory as far as it goes. Next, as to those shameful debts. You must pay them instantly. Has Angelica given you the money? .

DAM. Yes; but it's gone.

MRS. B. (*excitedly*). Gone!

DAM. (*correcting himself*). I mean gone by mail. I paid the bills on the spot.

MRS. B. Oh! I'm glad you have had that sense of honor. And now to the most important point.

DAM. Is there another point?

MRS. B. (*intently, leaning forward*). The uncle!

DAM. What uncle?

MRS. B. The uncle who called you to account for the fate of his niece.

DAM. Oh! Oh, he's all right. He'll cool down. (*Aside.*) What a mess of rubbish I made up.

MRS. B. I cannot believe it. My child's happiness is at stake, and that man must be conciliated.

DAM. But, my dear Mrs. Babbitt, —

MRS. B. Don't try to put me off. My resolve is taken. I must communicate with that man, and entreat his pardon, for the sake of my innocent daughter whom you have married.

DAM. (L.). It's not at all necessary. I beg you won't feel the slightest uneasiness.

MRS. B. (*shaking her head obdurately*). I shall write. I this very night. Give me his address.

DAM. (L., *aside*). Here's a pretty kettle of fish! (*Aloud.*) I cannot give you his address.

MRS. B. Why not?

DAM. I don't know it.

MRS. B. His last address.

DAM. He's changed it. He skips about from place to place.

MRS. B. He is searching for you.

DAM. What nonsense! I assure you, he's quite satisfied. As long as the bills are paid, he'll let up.

MRS. B. How will he know that the bills are paid?

DAM. (*aside*). O Lord! (*Aloud.*) I shall tell him.

MRS. B. You don't know his address.

DAM. I didn't say I would write to him. I said I would tell him.

MRS. B. You know where to find him?

DAM. (*exhausted*). No. (*Savagely.*) The fact is, I have told him.

> [*READY* SNAP, *with MSS.*, *and* PROFESSOR, *to enter* L.

MRS. B. (*alarmed*). He has been here?

DAM. Quite casually. Travelling to see the university. (*Crosses to* R.)

MRS. B. (L.). I have a dreadful apprehension! Those high words I heard just before I entered —

DAM. No, no! We parted on the best of terms.

MRS. B. You assure me sacredly that you are reconciled?

DAM. Sacredly.

MRS. B. (*hand to her heart*). Oh, what a relief! Go instantly and reassure your wife. You don't know in what a state I left her. (*Sinks into chair.*)

DAM. (*angrily*). I can imagine. (*Aside, going.*) Meddling old —! Confound it! it's my own fault. I'll never play another joke as long as I live. (*EXITS*, R., *in temper.*)

MRS. B. (*looks after him*). I believe he is truly repentant. (*Goes to door*, R., *and listens.*) If he is only kind to Angelica.

SNAP *RE-ENTERS*, L., *with MSS., followed by the* PROFES-SOR, *rubbing his hands. He perceives* MRS. BABBITT *instantly.*

PROF. My wife ! Great Scott ! (*Runs off,* L.)
SNAP. His wife ! (*Tries to steal towards door,* C.)
MRS. B. (R., *rises, turns and sees him*). A stranger !
                                    [*He stops awkwardly.*
Who are you ? What are you doing ?
SNAP. Nothing, nothing in particular, my dear madam !
Mrs. Babbitt, I believe ?
MRS. B. (R.). Are you looking for my husband ?
SNAP. No, no. Not at all.
MRS. B. Or the doctor ? Shall I call him ?
SNAP. Pray don't. I don't want the doctor. I'm quite well, thank goodness ! I've had enough of the doctor.
MRS. B. (*alarmed*). You — you have seen my son-in-law, then ?
SNAP. Yes; it's all right. I bear no malice. (*Aside.*)
Barn-stormers, indeed !
MRS. B. (*aside and in alarm*). No malice ! Good heavens !
can it be the uncle ? (*Aloud.*) You — you are a stranger ?
SNAP (*quickly*). Yes, a traveller ! Stopped over to see the — university.
MRS. B. (*aside*). It is he !
SNAP (*trying to escape*). I wish you good-morning.
MRS. B. Stop ! (*Breathlessly.*) Concealment is useless.
I know your business here. Before you go you and I must have an explanation.
SNAP (*aside*). She wants to get the play back. (*Puts MSS. in his breast pocket and buttons up.*) Not if I know it.
MRS. B. (*approaching with sympathy*). I know all.
SNAP (*defiantly*). Well, if you know all, you know that

things have gone too far to have any fooling now. (*Crosses to* R.)

MRS. B. (*draws him gently forward*). No one — no one sympathizes with your poor niece more than I do.

SNAP (R.). Niece! I have no niece.

MRS. B. No; because you heartlessly cast her off.

SNAP. 'Gad, it's a regular play. (*Strikes an attitude.*) Ay, I cast her off. What then? (*Aside.*) I'll let her play it out. (*Folds his arms and gazes at her.*)

MRS. B. And you have come to seek satisfaction from my son-in-law.

SNAP. Eh? Oh, have I? (*Aside.*) And I'll get it, too. Barn-stormers! Ha! ha! (*Aloud.*) What would you? (*Strikes a gloomy attitude.*)

MRS. B. He has wronged you.

SNAP (*naturally*). In my tenderest point.

MRS. B. Oh, how you must have suffered when the convent gates closed upon that broken-hearted child!

SNAP (*pretends to be shaken with emotion, and aside, turning from her*). It's a regular Seaside Library dramatized! She's given me the cue, though. That young villain, to deceive a broken-hearted girl! I'll pile some more on him. (*Aloud and à la* Iago.) You don't know all! Have you courage?

[*READY* DAMASK *and* ANGELICA, *to enter* R.

MRS. B. (*firmly*). I am his mother-in-law.

SNAP. The niece was not his only victim!

MRS. B. Great heavens! (*With intense curiosity.*) Go on!

SNAP (*crosses to* C.). Poor, poor Camille! (*Handkerchief to eyes.*)

MRS. B. I shudder at your words.

SNAP. One day the old man came home — the girl's father, I mean. He came home to — to dinner. (MRS. BABBITT *drops into chair.*) It was too late! They had flown, leaving a note upon his empty plate.

MRS. B.   And the end, the end?

SNAP.   For years that wronged father pursued the search for his only Camille.   At length he found his child in wretched lodgings, abandoned to the care of pampered menials.   The ruffian had deserted her.   His paltry reason, her want of grammar.   (*Stage*, L.)

MRS. B. (*rises*).   The upstart!   It is just like him.

DAMASK *RE-ENTERS with* ANGELICA, R.

So, sir!

SNAP.   The deuce!   (*Tries to bolt.* MRS. BABBITT *holds him.*)

DAM.   By Jove!   (*Tries to push* ANGELICA *off again.*) This is no place for you.

MRS. B.   Stay where you are.   I have had an interview with the uncle.   He has told me all.

DAM.   What, Snap?   (*Aside.*)   How clever of him to take the part at a moment's notice!   (*Crosses to him; aloud.*) My dear sir!   (*Aside.*)   I owe you more than I can pay.

SNAP (*aside*, L.).   I'm afraid you do.

MRS. B. (R. C.).   So, sir — there was another victim!

ANG.   Mamma!   (*Coming forward.*)   Another victim!

DAM.   Another vic—!   (*Drops* SNAP'S *hand.*)

MRS. B.   He has revealed to me the full measure of your wickedness.

ANG.   O Henry!

MRS. B.   What have you done with Camille?

[*READY curtain.*

ANG. (*shrieks*).   Camille!   (*Crosses to* R. C.)

DAM.   Cam—!   (*To* SNAP.)   You—!

ANG.   Mother!   Camille!   (*Screams.*)

[DAMASK *rushes to catch* ANGELICA.

MRS. B. (*interposes and waves him off*).   Monster!

[DAMASK *now makes a dart after* SNAP, *who has stood above, laughing.   The latter rushes for door, as the*

CURTAIN FALLS.

ACT III.

SCENE. — *Same as Act I. It is night; the lamps on the tables, R. and L., are lighted. A fire is burning in the grate.*

> *As the curtain rises the music of a brass band is heard playing such an air as they perform outside of country shows. NISBE is discovered seated at the fireplace. She holds a copy of " Life" in her hand, as if she had been reading. She jumps up as the music continues, and looks out of the window. READY* PROFESSOR, *to enter* L.

NISBE (*after music has played a few minutes*). I can see the lights at the theatre, and the band is playing to attract the people. (*Turning away from the window.*) Oh, if I could only go! But mamma knows nothing about our play, and wouldn't let me go if she did. (*Throws herself in seat by table,* C.) How will papa ever pass the evening? Here's his comic paper, and there's his easy-chair by the fire. (*Puts paper on table,* C.) But he won't rest content; I know he won't. (*Sits.*)

The PROFESSOR *ENTERS nervously from* L., *in old-fashioned full-dress suit, much too large. Looks out and then comes down shivering.*

PROFESSOR. Is that you, Nisbe?

NIS. Papa, do try and compose yourself. You are wandering up and down stairs so often that you will surely be suspected.

PROF. I can't compose myself.

NIS. Sit by the fire and read. (*Fixes chair for him up c.*) Here's *Life;* it's very funny this week. (*Offers paper.*) I laughed over it ever so much.

PROF. (*rejects paper*). I don't feel funny to-night. I feel like Guy Fawkes with his gunpowder, waiting for the clock to strike. (*Runs to window.*) I think I see the people go. ing to the theatre.

NIS. (*running to look, peeping over his shoulder*). Oh, it can't be! It wants a full hour before they begin.

PROF. (*looks at his watch, coming down, crosses to* R.). So it does. The minutes drag like hours.

NIS. (*takes his arm and leans her head on his shoulder*). O papa, if I could only go!

PROF. (R.). Do be sensible, child. It's no use. You know what your mother is. It's hard enough for me to steal off.

NIS. (L., *surprised*). Do you think of going?

                        [*READY* SUSAN, *to enter* L. C.

PROF. (*testily*). Of course. I must. Harry and I have made up a plan.

NIS. (*pouting*). Harry, too! I think your plan might take me in.

PROF. It can't. You see, we pretend that we've been asked to a whist party at the President's — nobody but men. Don't you let on.

NIS. (*nods, and then squeezes close to his arm*). I won't. Will the performance be very good, papa?

PROF. I don't know. I ran away from rehearsal to-day in misery. I never saw anything so bad. But Snap says it will be all right at night.

NIS. (L.). Of course it will, if he says so. Tell me all about the characters. Will Cassius be nice?

PROF. Oh, that's Mr. Chumley. He seems to be the best of the lot.

Nis. I knew from the first he'd be good. There's some-thing so superior about him; don't you think so? I declare, I could cry at not going. (*Crosses to* R.)

SUSAN *ENTERS*, L. C., *and calls in a whisper.*

SUSAN. Professor! Professor!

PROF. (*in whisper*). What is it?

SUSAN (*same, coming down*). The manager is here, and must see you.

PROF. (*alarmed*). What can he want? (*To* NISBE.) Where's your mother?

NIS. (*points* R.). In there with Harry and Angy.

[*READY* SNAP *and* JACK, *to enter* L. C.

PROF. Peep through the keyhole, and see if she stirs.

[NISBE *runs up to* R. D., *and obeys.* (*To* SUSAN.) Where have you got him?

SUSAN. In the vestibule. A young gentleman is with him. That Mr. Chumley.

NIS. (*looking up*). Cassius? Oh, let 'em come up, papa. Let Cassius come up.

PROF. (*to* NISBE). Sh! (*To* SUSAN.) Bring them in, but don't make a noise.

SUSAN (*creeping out on tip-toe*). All right, Professor! (*EXITS*, L. C.)

NIS. (*coming down*). You needn't be afraid, papa. Harry is reading out loud, and mamma and Angy are sewing.

PROF. (L., *relieved*). Very well. Now you go and keep them in there until I come.

NIS. (*pouts*). But I want to stay.

PROF. Go, I tell you. (*Goes to* L. C., *softly.*)

NIS. Just as he is here! But I'll find some excuse for coming back. (*Takes a bunch of keys out of her pocket, and after assuring herself that her father is not looking, she lays them on the mantel.*)

SUSAN *shows in* SNAP, L. C., *in long ulster, and* JACK. JACK *bows very politely to* NISBE, *who returns it and EXITS delightedly, at* R. SUSAN *EXITS*, L. C.

PROF. (R., *in low tone at first, and then naturally*). Now what is it? What's gone wrong? Will you have to postpone it?

SNAP. Postpone it! What an idea! Why, the house is sold out. It's the biggest thing I ever did.

PROF. If it were only over! I feel a cold chill through and through.

JACK (L.). Of course you do, my dear sir. But wait till we end in a burst of glory. That'll warm you.

PROF. (*crosses to* C., *shakes his hand*). Do you think so? (*To* SNAP.) But what are you doing here? You'll be late. You come on in the first act.

SNAP. Don't fret about me. I'll dress for King Titus Tatius in five minutes.

PROF. Then, what is it? What do you want?

SNAP (*scratches his head, embarrassed*). Well, the fact is, Professor, it's about the part of that confounded female slave.

PROF. My beautiful Sabine! Why, I altered it for your boy.

SNAP. Yes, but my wife has just remembered that everybody's on the stage in Tullia's scene, and we want him to do the tumult of citizens behind, and to ring down the curtain. We haven't another soul to spare.

PROF. (*in despair*). Then what's to be done?

JACK. Awful fix, isn't it?

SNAP. Don't lose your head. My wife's got an idea. (*Checking off on his fingers.*) You see Tullia cannot be a female slave, because we haven't a young woman left; it can't be a child, because he has got his hands full with the tumult.

JACK. And the curtain.

SNAP. So there's nothing left but to condense the whole part into a letter.

PROF. A letter ! (*Crosses to* R.)   Are you mad?

SNAP. Not at all.   We can have a messenger bring on a letter.   Cassius reads it.   You can keep in all the poetry, if you like, and you have the whole effect.

JACK (L.).   But you forget, we haven't any one to do the messenger.   That won't do. [*READY* SUSAN, *to enter* L. C.

SNAP (*nonplussed*).   That's a fact ! (*Suddenly.*)   Well, I'll tell you what.   You can find the letter on the stage. (*To* PROFESSOR.)   It's a wood scene.   The letter can be left on a stump before the curtain goes up.   (*To* JACK.   PRO-FESSOR *sinks into chair at table.*)   At the cue for the entrance of the female slave, you discover the letter, say " Ha ! what have we here ?   By all the gods, a letter ! " — and there you are.   Just practice that.

[JACK *does so up stage,* L., *gesticulating violently, and mutters as if acting.*

PROF. No, no !   It's absurd !   They'll guy it.   They'll howl at the whole thing.

SNAP. Not a bit !   We've done worse than that, and they stood it.   Just write the letter.   (*Pulls out MSS. and gives it to him.*)   We haven't anything to lose.   It'll be all right.   (*Pats him on back.*)

PROF. Do what you like with me; I'm prepared for any-thing.   (*Going,* L.)   I wish from the bottom of my heart I had never gone into the business.   (*EXITS,* L. D.)

SNAP (*following the* PROFESSOR, *winks back at* JACK.) Wait here.   I'll bring the letter !   (*EXITS,* L. D.)

JACK. Poor old gentleman !   He won't know his tragedy. (*Sits,* R.)

SUSAN *peeps in,* L. C., *and comes down cautiously to* JACK.

SUSAN. O Mr. Chumley, do tell me if anything is

wrong. I listened outside, but I couldn't make out more than a word here and there. I know it's about our play; isn't it?

JACK. Yes.

SUSAN. Won't it be played? Has anything happened to stop it? Break it softly to me; if you say "Yes," I'll fall right down where I stand.

JACK (R.). Calm yourself, Susan. Everything is going well. I've brought you your ticket. (*Gives it.*)

SUSAN. Oh, dear! "L. — 13–15!" Why, I'll melt there. I don't know yet how I'm to get over. Monday ain't my night out, and I never get an extra without a week's notice to Mrs. Babbitt. But I'd cut over and see it, if I was to get warning on the spot. I couldn't stay home with the excitement I'm in. Take my advice, Mr. Chumley, and never write a play; I can't tell you all the worry we've gone through with this one.

JACK. I assure you everything will be all right. (*Crosses to L.*)

SUSAN (*shakes her head*). I don't believe it! (*With emphasis.*) I don't believe it. I laid out the cards last night before I went to bed, and they came out unlucky every time. (*Mysteriously.*) The nine of spades turned up alongside the professor three times hand running. Ain't that a warning?

JACK (*laughs*). Is the nine of spades fatal?

SUSAN. Don't laugh, Mr. Chumley! Miss Nisbe used to laugh at the cards once, but you should see her now. I've seen her sitting at this here table (*indicating table*, R.) these three days telling her fortune with them. (*Opens drawer of table and produces cards.*) There they are now.

JACK (*anxiously*). Are you sure you delivered my bouquets to her every morning? [*READY* NISBE, *to enter* R. D.

SUSAN (R.). Every morning before breakfast!

JACK. What did she say?

SUSAN. Oh, she was furious!

JACK (*dejected*).   Furious?

SUSAN.   When she asked me who they were from and I told her, she scolded me awful.   How dare I do such a thing, and what did I mean by it.   (*Crosses to* L.)

JACK.   I was afraid of that.   What did she do with 'em?

SUSAN (*confidentially*).   She took them straight to her room and put them in water; and when they got faded she took 'em out and wrapped each one of 'em in tissue paper and put 'em away in her hat-box.

JACK (*overjoyed*).   Did she?   In her hat-box!   O Susan, if you knew how happy that makes me!   In her hat-box, too!   (*Crosses to* L., *rapturously*.)

NISBE *ENTERS*, R. D., *apparently looking for something.*

NISBE (*crossing to* C.).   Susan, did you see—   (*Sees* JACK.) Oh, I beg pardon!   Are you here still?

JACK.   Yes, quite still, thank you; I'm waiting for the professor.

NIS.   Indeed!   Susan, have you seen my keys?

[SUSAN *is about to look for them on the mantel.* No, no.   They can't be here.   I must have. left them in the laundry, or in the storeroom.   Go and see.   If they are not there they must be in the cellar.   (*Crosses to* R.)   I was down there to-day.   (*Pretends to look about room.*)

SUSAN.   Yes, Miss Nisbe. · (*Going.*)

JACK (*aside, to* SUSAN).   Susan!   Stay in the cellar as long as you can.

SUSAN (*nods and smiles, and looks at both; then when in the doorway*).   O Miss Nisbe!   If I can't find them in the cellar, shall I look in the garret?

NIS.   Yes, yes; only go at once.

SUSAN (*aside*).   I'll just stay outside the door and listen. I'm too fond of this sort of thing to lose a syllable. (*EXITS*, L. C.)

NIS. (*feeling in her pocket and looking around*).   I can't think!   [*They change sides, looking away from each other.*

JACK.   May I help you search?

NIS. (L.).   Thank you, Susan will find them.   Won't you sit down? (*Sits.*)

JACK.   If you will permit me.   (*Short pause.   Both much embarrassed; finally.*)   Oh! (*She starts.*)   I beg pardon, but I have suddenly remembered that I have a favor to ask of you.

NIS.   Of me?

JACK.   I see a pack of cards on the table.   My sisters used to tell fortunes with cards.   Do you understand the art?

NIS. (*eagerly*).   Oh, yes!   I know it very well!

JACK.   I am not generally superstitious, you know, but there are moods in which we long to question fate.

NIS. (*half to herself*).   Oh, yes; I know.   I've felt 'em myself.

JACK.   I will confess to you that I am at this moment at the turning-point of my life.   I'm meditating a step — (*Getting to* C.)

NIS.   A step?

JACK.   A step (*drops in chair*) on which the happiness or unhappiness of my future depends.   If you would give me but a hint.

NIS. (*pretending innocence*).   How?

JACK.   I mean by the cards.   Please read for me in my book of fate.   (*Hands her the cards.*)

NIS.   I'll try.   (*Crosses to* R.   *She looks around, as if in search of something.   He looks around too.   She looks the reverse way.   They turn round and bump.   He turns to her in comic surprise.*)   I want something to hold on my lap — a big book or something.   (*Crosses to* L.)

JACK (*brings chair forward, and takes up portfolio from table,* R.)   Will this do?   [NISBE *places chair for herself.*

NIS.   Yes, thank you.

[*He brings it; he sits before her, and they place it on
their knees together.*

That will do. (*She shuffles cards.*) You see, first I shuffle
them. That is important. (*Lays them down.*) Now, you
must cut.

JACK. I beg your pardon! Eh? Oh, the cards! I
thought you meant — (*Cuts cards.*)

NIS. There, so! Now I divide them into four parts, and
lay each part down so. (*Does so.*) Now, you must make a
wish.

JACK (*looking up rapturously*). I have made a wish!

NIS. (*looks through one of the piles and finds the king of
hearts, and holds it before him.*) Remember that card, that
is you.

JACK. The king of hearts — I see.

NIS. Yes, because you are light.

JACK. Light? Ah, light-headed — I mean light-hearted.

NIS. (*spreads out the pile in which the king is*). And these
are your thoughts.

JACK. And what am I thinking of?

NIS. (*shakes her head at them*). Nothing serious. (*Puts her
finger on one meditatively.*) Here is a passing fancy! (*Finger
on another.*) And here is an early separation which you find
it hard to get over. (*Lays king aside.*)

JACK. Oh, that must be a mistake.

NIS. (*gathers up the first pile and lays it aside. Takes up
another*). Now, pay attention. (*Deals them face up and
counts.*) 1, 2, 3, 4, 5, 6, 7. (*Picks out card.*) An old gentleman. (*Lays card alongside of king of hearts.*)

JACK. That's my stern parent.

NIS. (*takes up another pile and counts*). 1, 2, 3, 4, 5, 6, 7.

JACK. Seven again!

NIS. (*ruminating on seventh card*). That's bad! (*Cheerfully.*) But it doesn't amount to much. (*Puts pack down.*)

JACK. I'm glad of that.

Nis. (*third pile, same bus.*).   1, 2, 3, 4, 5, 6, 7.   An important letter.

Jack.   Oh, that's the letter we sent to make up with the dear old gentleman.

Nis. (*fourth pile, counting*).   1, 2, 3, 4, 5, 6, 7.   An unsettled, light young man.

Jack.   That must be I.

Nis. (*returns to first pile*).   1, 2, 3, 4, 5, 6, 7.

Jack.   Quick was the little maid's reply, "O master, we are seven!"   'Hem!   Wordsworth.

Nis.   A fair young woman!   (*Goes back over the cards in her hand.*)   And a temporary illness.   It looks like a fainting spell.

Jack.   But that doesn't amount to much.

Nis. (*places the card in the row with the others*).   The young woman is very near you.   [*READY* Susan, *to enter* L. C.

Jack (*moving the card*).   Put her a little nearer.

Nis. (*raps his hand; he withdraws it, and she moves the card back.   Then takes up the third pile and counts*).   1, 2, 3, 4, 5, 6, 7.   There is a change taking place in you.

Jack.   There is; I feel it.

Nis. (*running over the pile*).   And in the young lady. (*Holds up a card in artless surprise.*)   See!

Jack (*seizes her hand*).   Tell me about the young lady.

Nis. (*rises, shutting up book with the cards, and rising with the pile she has in her hand*).   No, I can't.   It's all nonsense.

Jack (*puts chair back*).   How can it be nonsense, when it's just commencing to be interesting?   (*Goes to her.*)   Come, do go on.   1, 2, 3, 4, 5, 6, 7.   What about the young lady?

[*READY* Snap, *with M.S.S. and sheet of paper, to enter* L.

Nis. (*crosses to* R.; *breaks away*).   Oh, I — I can't tell you that!

Jack (*following her*).   Oh, you must!   I can't give that seven up.

Nis. Well, then. (*Opening cards.*) 1, 2, 3, 4, 5, 6, 7. Oh,
I can't! (*Dashes off,* R., *leaving the cards in his hand.*)

Jack. She runs off and leaves my fate in darkness. (*Opens
cards.*) If I only knew what she thought that card meant!

Susan, L. C., *puts her head in door, up stage.*

Susan. How far have you got?

Jack. 1, 2, 3, 4, 5, 6, 7. I say, Susan, come here. Here's
a young lady with a change coming over her! Seven's the
change, I suppose. Seven's the nine of hearts! (Susan *holds
up both hands.*) What does the nine of hearts mean?

Susan. Don't you know? That's luck! The young lady
loves you!

Jack. Loves me! Does she? (*Hugs* Susan.) I'm overjoyed.

Susan (*looking up archly, as he's about to kiss her*). I'm
not the young lady, am I?

[*READY* Damask, *to enter* R.; *and* Professor, *with
pen, to enter* L.

Jack. No, but I'm so happy!

Snap *ENTERS,* L., *with the MSS. and with a sheet of paper,
on which is writing.*

Snap. Hello! Hello!

[Susan *breaks away and goes into alcove, dusting vigorously.* Jack *turns and claps* Snap *on both shoulders, and pulls him to and fro in his ecstasy.*

Jack. Snap, my boy, she loves me! 1, 2, 3, 4, 5, 6, 7! She
loves me! (*Flourishing card.*)

Snap (*seizing him by the arm*). For Heaven's sake, don't
go off your head at this critical moment. Come, we must go
to the theatre. It's eight o'clock!

Jack. No! It's 1, 2, 3, 4, 5, 6, 7 o'clock, Snap! But, no
matter, what's an hour more or less when you're in paradise?
In paradise, Snap! In paradise! (*Drags him off,* L. C.)

SUSAN (*comes down*). Eight o'clock! The theatre begins at eight, and I am still in this dress. (*Takes off apron.*) I'll just throw my cloak on and run over, let 'em scold as much as they like. I'll have to-night to myself, if they bounce me to-morrow. (*Runs out,* L. C.) [*READY* NISBE, *to enter* R.

DAMASK *ENTERS,* R., *and speaks off with great politeness.*

DAMASK. Only a moment, mamma. I'll be back directly. (*Comes down petulantly.*) This is a pretty piece of business!

PROFESSOR *ENTERS,* L., *wiping his pen on his coat-sleeve, hurriedly.*

PROF. Well, did you propose it?

DAM. Yes; and she won't let us go.

PROF. Did you tell her the president of the college asked us particularly to meet somebody?

DAM. She insists upon our staying at home this evening. It appears that she is feeling particularly amiable, and she wants to make it a peace celebration. She and Angy are in a state of emotional tenderness.

PROF. That's horrible! (*Trots to window.*) Look at all the people streaming to the theatre. They'll begin the play very soon.

DAM. (*looking over his shoulder*). By Jove, it's exciting! Makes you want to jump out of the window!

PROF. (*irritated*). And we have to stand here caged, like two children. (*Shows tickets.*) Look, here are our seats.

NISBE *ENTERS from* R., *cautiously, and closes door softly after her.*

DAM. What's the use of tickets? She won't let us out. What is to be done? I can't think of anything.

NIS. (*coming forward*). I'll tell you.

PROF. Nisbe!

DAM. (C.). You?

NIS. (*crosses to* C., *between them, finger to lips*).   I'll help you to get away — both of you.   But on one condition.

BOTH.   Yes, yes!

NIS.   You must take me with you.

PROF.   But your mother!

> [*READY* MRS. BABBITT *and* ANGELICA, *with work-baskets, to enter* R.

DAM.   How will you manage it?

NIS.   It's the easiest thing in the world, if you can go through with it.   When mamma comes in you, papa, must commence to find fault with me; it doesn't matter about what.   Then I'll give you saucy answers.   Then you get very angry with me, and send me to your room for the rest of the evening.   I go out crying; you lock me in.   I run down the back stairs, laughing, and wait for you on the stoop.

PROF.   Yes — that's all very well for you, but *we — we !*

DAM.   Yes, that gets you out all right —

NIS.   Sh!   As soon as I leave the room you, Harry, you take my part.   Get into a dispute with papa about his ill-treating me — both of you get heated!   You (*to* DAMASK) take up your hat at being insulted, and run out of the house — and join me!

DAM.   Splendid!

PROF.   Yes, but where do I come in?

NIS.   Why, you seize your hat and run after Harry, to find him, apologize, and bring him back.

DAM.   Glorious!   (*Hugging her.*)   Nisbe, you're a witch!

PROF.   Children, it's a very good scheme, but it won't work.   (*Goes up shaking his head, and takes a peep out of the window.*)

MRS. BABBITT *and* ANGELICA *ENTER at* R.   *They bring their work-baskets, as if to make themselves comfortable for the evening.*   ANGELICA *arranges chairs at the fire.*   MRS. BABBITT *goes to* PROFESSOR, *who comes from window as soon as he sees her.*

MRS. BABBITT. Mr. Babbitt! Justinian! Has Harry told you that I wish to make this evening an occasion of family reunion?

PROF. Yes, unfortunately.

MRS. B. We must forgive Angelica's husband. True, his past life has been a stormy one, but he repents, and we have pardoned. Have we not, Angelica?

ANGELICA. Yes, mamma, with all our hearts. (*She embraces* DAMASK, *who has come to her after a brief pantomime aside with* NISBE.)

DAM. My darling!

MRS. B. And, henceforth, no more mystery.

DAM. (*crosses to her and back, embraces and kisses her*). No, mamma.

MRS. B. (*to* PROFESSOR). And you, Justinian, you will be your own old self again, won't you, darling? No more abstraction, no fits of silence, no long absences, morning, noon, and night.

PROF. (*absently*). Certainly! Certainly! (*She embraces him rapturously and kisses him.*)

MRS. B. Children, this is a happy evening for us all.

PROF. *and* DAM. (*looking at each other dolefully.* PROFESSOR *embraces* MRS. BABBITT. DAMASK *embraces* ANGELICA. *He and* PROFESSOR *wink at each other*). Yes, very!

MRS. B. (*sitting at fire and arranging her work*). We'll have a nice cosey time together.

PROF. (*looking at his watch, coughing, and looking from* NISBE *to* DAMASK, *who urge him on*). The fact is, Zippy, I wanted to go to the president's for a little while; he expects a friend, Professor Polhemus, from New York, this evening.

MRS. B. You can call on him to-morrow.

PROF. *and* DAM. (*quickly*). Oh, no! To-morrow won't do — never'll do!

MRS. B. (*decisively*). You will stay at home this evening.

We can't afford to spoil our family party for Professor Pol-hemus.

[*Both men subside.* PROFESSOR *at* L., DAMASK *at* R.

PROF. (*aside*). That won't work. (*Sits at table,* L.)

NIS. (*at window*). Oh, dear! (*Sighs loudly.*) It's an awful bore! (*Comes forward.*)

MRS. B. (*looks round*). What's that?

ANG. Why, Nisbe!

NIS. (*coming down,* C.). I said it was a bore to be cooped up every evening like this, at home. (*Aside, to* PROFESSOR.) Now get mad.

[PROFESSOR *turns to look at her.* DAMASK *motions to him.*

MRS. B. Well, I declare!

NIS. It's worse than a boarding-school. (*Aside, to* PRO-FESSOR.) Go on. Get mad!

MRS. B. Mr. Babbitt, do you hear your daughter?

PROF. (*rises, pulling himself together*). Sophonisba! I — I — don't quite understand you!

NIS. (*aside*). More! More!

PROF. Your tone and manner. (*Looks at watch, and goes up to window.*)

NIS. I don't know what papa has against me to-night. (*Sits in chair,* C., *pretending to cry.*) Only a few minutes ago I asked him, in the most casual manner, whether it was true that the Hindoos burn their mothers-in-law on the eve of marriage (MRS. BABBITT *starts up*), and he flared up and wanted to send me out of the room.

PROF. Nisbe, how dare you?

NIS. But I'm no longer a child, and I won't stand such treatment. (*Goes* L.)

DAM. (*aside,* R., *to* PROFESSOR). Now give it to her.

MRS. B. Sophonisba!

PROF. (*working himself into wrath*). Oh, ho! You won't stand it, eh? We'll see! Go to your room this instant!

no, go to mine, and don't show yourself again this evening. (NISBE *blubbers*.) Do you hear, miss? Go! (*to others*) and nobody's to go near her. We'll see whether you'll stand it.

MRS. B. (R. C., *expostulating*). But, my dear —

NIS. (*crossing, pretending to cry, but aside*). Go on; don't let up on me!

ANG. O papa! (MRS. BABBITT *and* ANGELICA *come down*.)

PROF. (*waving them off*). March! Go to my room!

NIS. (*sobbing violently*). Such treatment! in this house! oh! oh! oh! (*EXITS*, L. D., *sobbing*.)

ANG. (*crosses to* L. C.). Poor Nisbe!

PROF. (*pretending fury*). What business have you to interfere? [ANGELICA *goes to* MRS. BABBITT.

DAM. (L., *pretending anger*). Stop, Mr. Babbitt! Let's have no more of this. It's no concern of mine, perhaps, how you treat Nisbe; but when you insult my wife —!

PROF. Hold your tongue!

MRS. B. Justinian!

PROF. You, too!

MRS. B. Why, what has come over you?

PROF. (*lashing himself into a fury*). You are all leagued together. Whenever I am really and truly comfortable, and promise myself a peaceful evening at my own fireside, you drive at me like a nest of hornets, on the least provocation. But, very well! (*Seizes his hat and coat, winks at* DAMASK, *aside.*) Very'well! If I can't open my mouth in my own house — if I'm driven out like an interloper, I'll go! I won't 'be in your way any longer! I'll go!

[DAMASK *runs up to* PROFESSOR, *and tries to pass him.*

DAM. Me first!

PROF. No, no; you look out for yourself.

DAM. But —

PROF. I'll go! (*EXITS*, L. C.)

[DAMASK *drops into chair despondently.*

MRS. B. (C.).   Children, what is the matter with him?

ANG. (C.).   It's terrible!

MRS. B.   Where has he gone?   What will become of him?

DAM.   I had better look after him.   Who knows what may happen!   Angy, where's my hat?

ANG.   Here!   (*Gets it for him from table*, C.)

MRS. B.   Run quickly; he may get out of sight!

DAM.   No fear!   I'll find him.   (*EXITS*, L. C.)

MRS. B. (*sinks in chair at* L. *table*).   Oh!

ANG. (*in seat*, R.).   Was anything ever so dreadful!—and so sudden!

MRS. B.   These men are perfectly senseless.

ANG. (*on her dignity*).   You refer only to papa, I suppose. My husband shows his goodness of heart by running after him.

MRS. B.   Your husband shouldn't have meddled with him at first, and things wouldn't have gone so far.

ANG.   That's very unjust, mamma!   Harry's the most generous of men.

MRS. B.   Of course!   Especially when he runs up bills he can't pay, for some unworthy creatures.

ANG. (*hotly*).   You forgave him, and promised never to speak of it again.   (*Rises and goes up to sofa*, C.)   I couldn't have believed it of you.

MRS. B.   Don't bother me.   I don't wish to have any more words on the subject.

ANG.   Nor I.   (*Picks up* " Life," *and opens it.*)

MRS. B. (*during a short pause which follows, exhibits petu-lance, anger, and depression. Fidgets, and is altogether nervous; suddenly*).   Ugh!

ANG. (*who has been reading* "Life," *makes an outcry*). Well, I—!   (*Then starts up, still reading paper.*)   Mamma!

MRS. B. (*drops her work and turns*).   What is it?

ANG.   This is monstrous!   (*Comes down to* MRS. BAB

BITT.)   We have been deceived! — outraged! They are laughing at us.

MRS. B.   Who?   What?

ANG.   Papa and my husband.   It was a trick.

MRS. B.   What do you mean?

ANG.   Here's the whole thing in this paper.   Listen to it.   (*Reads.*)   "When our old friend Slyboots wishes to have a night out without his wife, he concocts a little plot with his son-in-law.   At a given signal, the latter asserts that it is the practice of the Hindoos to burn their mothers-in-law on the eve of their marriage."

MRS. B.   (*appalled*).   Angelica!

ANG.   (*reading*).   "Slyboots disputes the statement; the two gentlemen engage in a violent quarrel, in the course of which Mr. Slyboots pretends to get so enraged that he snatches up his hat and runs out of the house, and his son-in-law follows to apologize."   Just as papa did.

MRS. B.   It's an outrage!   A conspiracy!

ANG.   Of course!   You remember how papa flared up at Nisbe without reason?

MRS. B.   To be sure.   And he sent the poor child out of the room.

ANG.   My dear innocent sister!

MRS. B.   (*calling off, room* L.).   Nisbe! Nisbe, darling! Come here, my child.   (*EXITS,* L. D.)

ANG.   (*calling off, also*).   You needn't stay there any longer.   Come and sit with us.

MRS. BABBITT *RE-ENTERS after a shriek.*

MRS. B.   Angelica!   There's no one in the room.   She's gone.

ANG.   It can't be, mamma!   (*Rushes off,* L. D.)

MRS. B.   The back door's open, too!

ANGELICA *RE-ENTERS.*

ANG.   She has run off.

MRS. B. (*screams*).   Now, I think of it!

ANG. (L.).   What, mamma?

MRS. B. (R.).   Nisbe is in the plot.

ANG.   True!   It was she commenced about the Hindoo mothers-in-law.

MRS. B.   Oh, the wretched child!

ANG.   Deceitful husband!

MRS. B.   Your conscienceless father!

ANG. (*half weeping*).   And Harry promised me on this spot, not ten minutes ago, never to tell me an untruth again. Mamma, this breaks my heart!   (*In her arms.*)

MRS. B.   My poor child!   Chained for life to a man who begins by deceiving you.   You are, indeed, to be pitied.

[*READY* MULBERRY, *to enter* L. C. *with* ANGELICA.

ANG.   No, mamma!   You are most to be pitied.   To have papa end by deceiving you.   Poor mamma!

MRS. B.   My poor daughter!   (*They embrace.*)

[*The door-bell is heard to ring.*

ANG.   There's the front door-bell.

MRS. B. (*becoming rigid and sarcastic*).   Ah! They're coming back!

ANG. (*stiffening up*).   We'll give them the reception they deserve!   [*Bell rings again.*

MRS. B.   Why doesn't Susan open the door?

ANG. (*runs to* L. C., *and calls*).   Susan!   (*Listens, and then calls again.*)   Susan!   (*Turns.*)   Susan's gone out, too.

[*Bell.*

It's as good as a play.   [*Bell again.*

MRS. B.   What is going to happen next?

ANG.   I'll open the door myself.   (*EXITS*, L. C.)

MRS. B.   I'll remember this night as long as I live! (*Listens*, L. C.)

MULBERRY (*outside*).   Professor Babbitt!

ANG. (*outside*).   My father?

MRS. B.   A strange voice!

ANGELICA *RE-ENTERS, preceding, in some alarm,* LORD
MULBERRY, *who is over polite.   Both ladies much
frightened.*

A stranger!   What do you wish, sir?   (*She and* ANGELICA
cling together.)

MULBERRY (L.).   Excuse me, ladies, I'm looking for Professor Babbitt.

MRS. B.   My husband!   I'm sorry he's not in.

MUL.   My name is — ahem — Mulberry.

MRS. B.   Mul —

ANG.   Berry.

MUL.   From England.   At present stopping in New
York.

MRS. B.   I'm very glad to see you.   (*Recovering, and aside
to* ANGELICA.)   He seems to be a gentlemanly person.

ANG. (*aside,* R.).   Yes, but he is so queer.   Look how he
smiles and stares at us.

MUL.   Your husband, no doubt, has told you a great deal
about my affairs.

MRS. B. (*sardonic laugh*).   My husband never tells me
anything.   I have to find out everything by chance.

MUL. (*aside*).   Singular person!   The Professor described
his wife as possessing remarkable sweetness of manner.
(*Aloud.*)   Strictly speaking, I came to see your son-in-law,
Dr. Damask.

ANG. (*crosses to him, advancing a step*).   My husband?

MUL.   Oh, he's your husband!   Well, I've just come
from your house.   They told me he was here.

ANG. (*dryly*).   I'm sorry.   He's not in, either.

MUL.   And I am sorry, very sorry.

ANG.   If you wish to consult him — his office hours are
from five to six.   It's now after eight.

MUL. (*aside*).   She seems to be a little excited, too.

Takes after her mother, probably. (*Aloud.*) Excuse me.
ladies; as I haven't much time to spare, I'll go after the
gentlemen.   Where can I find them?

MRS. B. (*shrugs her shoulders*). We don't know.

MUL. And when will they be back?

ANG. (*crosses to* C.). We don't know that, either.

MUL. (*aside*). A most singular family. (*Aloud.*) Then
there's nothing left but to wait for them. (*Sits.*) I don't
intrude, do I?

MRS. B. (*crosses to* C., *as* ANGELICA *again clings to her*).
But, what do you want? (*She speaks tremblingly.*)

    [*The terror of the two ladies must not be exaggerated.*

MUL. (*affected*). It's about my misguided son. The Professor told you all about him?

MRS. B. Not a word! (*To* ANGELICA.) The man's an
impostor; we must get rid of him. (*Gets behind* ANGELICA.)

MUL. (*at table, seated,* L., *to* ANGELICA). The doctor told
you, of course?

ANG. He did not.

MUL. (*rising. Severely to both*). That is incomprehen-
sible to me. The doctor wrote me a letter four pages long
about the scamp.   I received it yesterday, and flew here to
see the boy.

MRS. B. Indeed! (*Aside, to* ANGELICA.) We haven't a
soul to send for a policeman.

MUL. You must know that the rascal has played the
most incredible pranks.   For two years I haven't heard a
word of him.   And now your husband writes me that he is
in this place, reduced to extremity, and praying for pardon.
(*Deeply affected and sinking in chair.*) My poor Jack!

ANG. (*aside, to* MRS. BABBITT). I'll slip out, mamma, and
call a neighbor.

MRS. B. Don't leave me! (*Grasps her.*)

MUL. (*to* MRS. BABBITT). I knew how it would end. He
began by a series of low attachments; first with one public

character and then another. Wasted his time, his money, his friends, and my patience. Collected a number of rings, photographs, and unpaid bills.

MRS. B. (*suddenly interested*). What?

MUL. Ruined himself, and finally bolted to America. (*Crosses to* R.)

ANG. (*open stage*). Mamma, this case is exactly like Harry's!

MUL. (*crosses to* C. *between the two; produces the pocket-book of Act II.*). You doubt it; look here! Evidence furnished by himself.

ANG. (*screams*). Gracious heavens! Harry's pocket-book.

MRS. B. How did you come by this?

MUL. It belongs to my son. He sent it to me through your daughter's husband.

MRS. B. (*appalled*). Oh!

ANG. Are you sure?

MUL. Oh, I can verify the vouchers. (*Opens book and produces articles.*) Here's a picture of my son's enchant-ress. I've seen the hussy. (*Puts photo on table.*) Here's a lock of her hair. She wears a wig now. Her ring. And here are the bills I'm going to pay. (*Crosses to* R.)

ANG. Mamma, did you hear?

MRS. B. With our money!

ANG. (*to* MRS. BABBITT). My husband invented another falsehood. Palmed somebody's adventures off for his own! (*Struck.*) Unless — (*Seizes* MULBERRY.) Is my husband your son? (*Turns away bewildered, up stage.*) Oh, no, no! This is madness.

MUL. (*looks at both astonished*). It certainly is. (*Crosses to* C.)

MRS. B. (L., *takes up the photo*). But I saw and spoke with the uncle of that girl.

MUL. Uncle! (*Takes the photo.*) She never had an uncle. (*Puts articles in pocket-book.*)

Ang.　Another falsehood! (*Throws herself into chair.*)

Mrs. B. (*in chair*).　To make a fool of me before a stranger!

Ang.　O mother!　　　　　[*READY* Nisbe, *to enter* L. C.

Mrs. B.　My poor child!

Mul. (*looks at both with a knowing air*).　They begin to make me feel uncomfortable.　Something's wrong here. (*Retreating nervously up* C.)　Excuse me, ladies.　Had I seen that the story of my misguided Jack would have excited you so —

Ang. (*starts up furiously*).　What do we care for your Jack?

Mrs. B. (*seizes* Mulberry).　One word!　Do you know Camille?

Mul.　Camille!　No; let me go! (*Tottering* C.)　I must get out of this, or I'll lose my reason!　It's a family of lunatics! (*EXITS*, L. C.) [*READY* Susan, *to enter* L. C.

Ang. (*resolutely, and striding across the room*).　Mamma! first of all, I'll get a divorce from Harry!　Open, persistent, and incessant falsehood must be sufficient cause.

Mrs. B.　Quite right, my child!　But he shall account to me first.　　　　　　　　　　　　　　　　　[*Bell heard.*

Ang. (*screams*).　Ah, there he is! (*Runs up*, C.)

Mrs. B.　Just in time! (*Crosses to* R.)

　　Nisbe *ENTERS*, L. C., *and rushes weeping into*
　　　　　　Angelica's *arms.*

Ang.　Nisbe! is it you?　　　　　[Nisbe *sobs.*

Mrs. B. (R.).　Where have you been?　　[Nisbe *sobs.*

Ang.　What has happened?　　　　[Nisbe *sobs.*

Mrs. B.　What are you crying for?

Nis. (*crosses to* C.).　Oh, it's horrible! (*Sobbing.*)　Let me be!　Let me be!

Ang.　Mamma, she's trembling all over.

Mrs. B.　What's the matter?

ANG. } (*together*).   Nisbe!
MRS. B. }   Speak, can't you?

> [*READY* DAMASK *and* PROFESSOR, *to enter* L. C.

NIS. (*sobs*). I can't! (*Sobs.*) Oh, it was dreadful! (*Outburst of sobs.*)

ANG. Mamma, she goes on as if she had seen something.

SUSAN, L. C., *first heard howling outside, now ENTERS.*

SUSAN. Oh, oh, oh! (*Throws herself in chair,* L., *rocking herself.*)

MRS. B. You, too; what is it? (*Crosses to her and back to* R.)

SUSAN. Oh, I can't tell you. It's too horrible.

NIS. (*crosses to* L. C.). O Susan, were you there?

SUSAN. I was! Oh, oh, oh!

NIS. Wasn't it awful? Oh, oh, oh!

ANG. Come, Nisbe! Come to your room! Tell me all!

NIS. (*is led off,* R.). Oh, oh! That I should live to see it! Oh, oh, oh! Poor papa! (*EXITS,* R., *with* ANGELICA.)

MRS. B. (*calls after them*). Put her to bed. (*To* SUSAN.) Run to the kitchen! Bring a cup of hot tea, quick!

SUSAN. Yes'm. Oh, oh! Poor Mr. Babbitt! Oh, oh, oh! Poor Professor! (*EXITS,* L. C.)

> [*READY* ANGELICA, *to enter* R.

MRS. B. What can it mean!   [NISBE *heard crying off* R. I'll get the hot drops! (*EXITS,* L.)

When the stage is empty, DAMASK *puts in his head,* L. C., *looks round, then puts off his hand and drags on the* PROFESSOR.

DAM. Now you're all right. Nobody here, fortunately.

PROF. (*staggers to seat,* C.). Harry, I can't walk! My knees are tottering.   [*He is led to seat,* C. Wasn't it terrible? (*Drops into chair.*)

DAM. Compose yourself. All may not be lost, if the audience did hiss a little in the first act.

PROF.   Hiss a little! At one time I thought sixty steam-pipes had burst upon me, all of a sudden, and all at once. No, no! my kind-hearted boy, you needn't try to console me! It wasn't the hissing; they laughed — laughed out loud at my tragedy!   [*READY* MRS. BABBITT, *to enter*, L. D.

DAM.   But, Professor —

PROF.   There was one boy in the gallery with a whistle; that whistle will vibrate in my ears till I die.

DAM.   Don't take it so to heart, and speak lower.   Courage! Hush! somebody's coming!

ANGELICA *runs in from* R.

ANG.   Mamma, where is the — (*Sees the others.*) Ah! (*Stands and stares at them.*)

DAM. (*crosses to her, affecting nonchalance, and with exaggerated kindness*).   Well, darling, what are you looking for?

ANG. (*looks at him from top to toe; then*).   I am looking for my mother, sir. (*EXITS*, L. C.)

DAM. (*stares after her, then turns to* PROFESSOR).   She's looking — for — her — mother!

PROF. (*rises*).   Sir!

DAM.   I don't like that look.

PROF.   Hush! my wife!   •

MRS. BABBITT *ENTERS hurriedly, from* L. D.

MRS. B.   Here are the drops! (*She has a small vial in her hand; sees them, and stops suddenly.*)   Oh!
          [*READY* SNAP, *to enter* L. C.

PROF. (*goes to her very affably*).   What drops, darling?

MRS. B. (*looks him all over*).   Drops for my daughter! (*Crosses to him.*)   But I'll see you again later, Mr. Babbitt; depend on that! (*EXITS*, R. D.)

PROF. (L.).   They know everything!

DAM.   What if they do?   What do they know?   What do *we know?*   Who knows how the play's gone on since we left?

You would bolt at the end of the first act. The others may go off like fireworks.

PROF. (*shakes his head very dubiously*). I think I hear them fizzing now.

DAM. Why, you said all along that all the acts were better than the first. Take that situation at the end of the second act. That must please the boys.

PROF. Not that boy with the whistle. (*Crosses to* R.)

DAM. Nonsense! Let's go back to the theatre and see. You may be called out!

PROF. Yes, by the police!

DAMASK *is about to lead him off*, L. C., *when* SNAP *is heard to utter a loud* "Oh!" *outside, a second one in the archway; he then comes forward in his long ulster, the collar turned up, and hat over his eyes.*

SNAP. O Professor! Professor, Oh!

PROF. Speak, man! What is it?

DAM. How is it going?

SNAP. It's all over! (*Lamenting, beating his head and knees.*) It's all over!

PROF. I knew it. (*Sinks.*)

[DAMASK *holds him up by the armpits.*

SNAP (*starting up*). When I think of this happening to me in my old age!

DAM. Tell us all about it.

SNAP. I've been a manager twenty-five years, but I never had such a failure as that.

PROF. (*feebly*). How did it end?

SNAP. How did it end? It ended in a riot! That's how it ended.

PROF. A — a — riot! (*Sinks in chair.*)

SNAP. We had to ring down in the middle of the second act. I never heard such hissing and whistling on a railroad train. The audience jumped up and down like madmen.

and shouted and guyed! I can hear 'em now, on my entrance, " Bully for Titus Tatius!"   Oh!

[*READY* Mrs. Babbitt, *to enter* R.

Prof. (*staggers to a seat*, C.).   It must have been horrible.

Snap.   But half the calamity was your fault, Doctor.   The
tragedy was not all to blame.   It was your parrot (*crosses to
him*) capped the climax.   The pine grove is in the second
act, you remember, and Cassius had just come on, and the
audience was quiet, for they took to him at once.   I was
standing in the centre, as King Titus Tatius, with my arms
folded, just so, glaring at the Roman soldiers, and my wife
had just finished Virgia's great speech, defying the haughty
Romulus : —

> "What would'st thou, king,
>   Thy stubborn silence break,
> What would'st thou,
> Tyrant! answer, speak!"

when your confounded parrot squeaked at the top of his
voice (*crosses to* L.): "Kiss me, darling." (Professor, *hor-
rified, starts up stage, sits on the steps, and buries his face in his
hands.*)   Of course that settled it.   The audience rolled off
their seats; the boxes emptied like one man, screaming with
laughter; and the gallery broke into a row, when my eldest
daughter had presence of mind enough to lower the curtain.
What has happened since I don't know, for I threw on my
ulster and fled through the stage door, and here I am.

Prof. (*rises*).   Oh, dear!   If it leaks out now that I
wrote the piece, I'll have to leave the town.

[*READY* Susan, *with tea and cups, to enter* L. C.

Dam.   Sh!   Mamma!

Snap.   The old lady!   The deuce!

Prof.   Not a word before her.

Mrs. Babbitt *ENTERS*, R.

MRS. B. Now, Mr. Babbitt. (*Sees* SNAP.) Ah, you are here again, are you? (*Looks at* DAMASK.) The uncle, I believe? (*Crosses* R. C. *To* SNAP.) Whose uncle?

[SNAP *advances to her.*

DAM. You are mistaken, mamma. This is quite another person.

MRS. B. (*to* DAMASK). I am quite aware of that, sir! Don't you interfere! (*To* SNAP.) Who are you, sir, and what do you want here?

SNAP (L. C.). Madame, I—

PROF. (*aside*, L.). Keep still!

DAM. I must interfere. You are laboring under a delusion. This is Professor Polhemus, from New York.

PROF. *first, and then* SNAP (*grasping at the idea*). Yes, Professor Polhemus, of New York.

DAM. You remember we were invited to meet him this evening.

SUSAN *ENTERS*, L.C., *with tea and cups, which she puts on table*, L.

SUSAN (*sobbing*). Here's the tea, ma'am.

MRS. B. Well, then, Professor Polhemus, from New York, make yourself at home. Take a cup of tea. (*Crosses to table*, L.)

[*READY curtain.*

PROF. *and* DAM. Yes, make yourself at home, Professor! (*Both assist him.*) Take off your coat. Give me your hat. Sit down, Professor.

[*As they unrobe him, he is discovered in full Roman costume,—white tunic, belt, fleshings, bare arms; but on his feet are old street gaiters.*

MRS. B. (*screams, and drops the cup she was about to offer him*). What's this?

[*Her screams bring* ANGELICA *and* NISBE *to door*, R. *and* C. *General dismay and*

QUICK CURTAIN.

ACT IV.

SCENE. — Same as Act III.

SNAP *is discovered asleep in the alcove at back, a large rug thrown over him. The* PROFESSOR *is writing at table,* L. *He looks very much disordered and played out. Is writing as the curtain rises.* READY SUSAN, *with breakfast on tray, to enter* L. C.

PROFESSOR (*laying down his pen*). That's done. I've asked for leave of absence from duty at the college. I could not face those boys.   [*Knock heard.* My wife! (*Goes to door,* R.) Is that you, Zippy?

SUSAN (*outside*). No; it's I, Professor. Open the door.

PROF. (*unlocks door*). What do you want?

SUSAN *ENTERS,* L. C., *bringing in tray, with breakfast.*

SUSAN. I've brought some breakfast, Professor. (*Puts tray on the table.*)

PROF. I don't want any breakfast.

SUSAN. That won't do. Look in the glass and see how haggard you are. Have a cup of coffee, anyway.

SNAP (*sitting up*). Might I ask for a cup, too?

SUSAN. Jiminy! What's that?

SNAP (*rises and comes down. Has on trousers and a coat much too small for him; no shirt, but the Roman breastplate in its stead*). Don't get frightened; it's only me.

SUSAN (R.). Why, Mr. Snap, what are you doing there?

SNAP. I've been stranded on the sofa all night, and the Professor helped me out with his wardrobe. I didn't dare to go home to my wife after that horrible fiasco.

SUSAN (*crosses* C. *to* PROFESSOR). Now, you haven't been in bed, either.

PROF. (L., *waking up*). I spent the night in that arm-chair.

SUSAN. It's awful! And you won't take breakfast?

PROF. I can't. I'm full now — of trouble.

SNAP. If you don't mind, I'll help myself. I must fortify myself against my first meeting with my wife. (*Pours out coffee, and eats,* R.)

PROF. (*aside*). I don't dare even think of my wife. (*To* SUSAN, *aside.*) Susan, has she given you any message?

SUSAN (C.). Nothing, sir. Oh, she's in such a rage! We all caught it last night. First, Miss Nisbe; then I. Missus talked to me as if I'd written the play myself, and it was all my fault. Well, I had my doubts when you were reading it. I like sad things at the theatre; but that was too sad. It was too miserable!

[*READY* JACK, *to enter* L. C.

SNAP. You don't know anything about it. If it hadn't been for that parrot! You'll see when we play it the second time.

PROF. You don't imagine for one moment I'd ever let the piece be played again?

SNAP. Why not? Let's talk calmly.

PROF. The manuscript shall be burnt; that settles it. I hope nobody in the city knows I'm the author.

SNAP. Rest easy. Nothing can be got out of my wife, and as for me —

PROF. I depend upon you. I quit town to-day, if I get the leave of absence I've written for.

SNAP. But, my dear Professor —

PROF. Not another word. I'm going to pack up my

things. Susan, bring my sole-leather trunk down from the garret. (*EXIT*, L. D.)

SUSAN (*sobbing and gathering the breakfast things together*). He was such a kind master, and to think the like should happen to him in his old days! (*EXIT*, L. C.)

JACK *ENTERS*, L. C., *hurriedly*.

JACK. Oh, there you are, at last! Been searching for you everywhere. I've a most important communication.

SNAP. If it's anything exciting, have the goodness to break it to me gently. I'm not toned up for a surprise.

JACK. My father arrived here yesterday. I spent the whole night with him, and we had a complete reconciliation. I shall leave for home with him to-day.

SNAP. How long a leave of absence do you want?

JACK. My dear fellow, it is not a question of leave of absence. I wish to tender my resignation, and say good-by to the stage forever.

SNAP (*utterly crushed, sinks back*). That — that was the only thing wanted. (*Starts up, but with difficulty, on account of his tight dress.*) You can't go — you are indispensable. (*Crosses*, L.) I don't refer to your talent, but to your unapproachably aristocratic wardrobe, and your nationality. I tell you, I've been a manager for twenty-five years, and I never had a leading man before with eight suits of clothes. How can we give a society play if you go off with your dress suit and your crush hat?

JACK. My dear Snap —

SNAP. No false modesty! Your things fit every one of the company like gloves. Even my wife made an immense hit as Nan, the Good for Nothing, in your velvet jacket.   ·

JACK. We can easily settle that objection. I'll leave you my theatrical wardrobe as a souvenir.

SNAP (*with feeling*). Mr. Chumley, you have not only a

true society manner, but a genuine respect for art. I admire you and I thank you.

JACK. That is not all. My father happens to own the ground upon which they put up the new Frivolity Theatre, in London.

SNAP. London! The birthplace of Shakespeare! Oh! —but go on.

JACK. If you release me gracefully, you shall be installed as manager.

[*READY* NISBE, *with large valise,· and* SUSAN, *with basket, to enter* L. C.

SNAP. Manager! In London! It has been the dream of my life to manage a theatre in London — or anywhere, for a whole season. You are discharged on the spot.

JACK. Well, then, it's settled?

SNAP. I should say so! But you must come with me to my wife; you must be there when I tell her about the theatre. You'll see what joy means. That unapproachable woman has borne our privations with resignation and courage, but I know that it has long been the secret hope of her heart to be able to stay in one place for more than "six nights only." Come, we'll go to her together.

JACK (*hesitating*). I'll follow you later. I'd like to say good-by to this family first.

SNAP. Very proper. The Professor is in there. (*Points,* L. D.)

JACK (*crosses to* L.). Thank you. I'll knock. (*Goes to door and is about to knock, when he hears* NISBE'S *voice.*)

NISBE (*outside*). This way, Susan. In here.

JACK (*aside*). Oh, there she is.

SNAP. Well, why don't you knock?

[JACK *imposes silence by a gesture as*

NISBE *ENTERS,* L. C., *with a large valise,* SUSAN *following with a basket.*

NISBE (*resting,* C.).   Put the basket down yonder.   (*Points down* R.)   I'll pack up by and by.

> [SUSAN *puts the basket down,* R., *and EXITS,* L. C.
> NISBE *puts the valise down near alcove,* R. C. ; *sees*
> SNAP.

Oh, pardon me, I'm looking for papa.

SNAP (*up* R.).   The Professor is in that room.   (*Points* L.)

NIS.   I suppose you are waiting for him.   I'll knock at his door.   (*Goes to* L., *and sees* JACK.)   O Mr. Cassius !

JACK (*gets quickly between her and the door*).   Please, Miss Nisbe, don't knock !

NIS.   Why not ?

JACK.   Wait here a little while — I mean — that is — you might disturb your father just now.   (*Comes from door.*)

SNAP (*officiously*).   Oh, no !   He's only packing up.   I'll knock.   (*Crosses to* C.)

> [*As he goes to door,* JACK *and* NISBE *get* R. *and* L. *of
> him, and keep him back.*

JACK (L.).   No, no !

NIS. (R.).   It's not at all necessary.

SNAP (C., *comprehends the situation.   Looks at both, chuckles, and then goes ; aside*).   Oh, I begin to see.   Act one, scene two — the lovers meet !   Everything in this house is as good as a play.   (*Aloud.*)   All right !   (*Crosses to* R.)   Don't be afraid.   I won't disturb the Professor.   It would be downright rude of me when you two are decidedly opposed to it.

JACK (*confused.   Waves him off, and takes* NISBE'S *hand*).   The fact is, Miss Nisbe, I have something very important to say to you.

NIS.   Is it very important ?

JACK (*warmly*).   I think so !

NIS. (*warmly*).   Really ?

JACK (*looks at his watch*).   And time is pressing.   The train leaves in two hours.   (*Crossing* C.)   I must leave for New York with my father by the twelve o'clock express.

NIS. (*crosses to* C.).   And I start for Boston with mamma at 12.20.   •

JACK (*looks at* SNAP *impatiently*).   Who knows when we may meet again?

NIS. (*crosses to* C., *looks at* SNAP *impatiently, then says sadly*).   Perhaps never.

SNAP (*bluntly*).   Then I should say the best thing would be to speak right out now.

JACK (*crosses to* C.).   But, my dear Snap, what I have to say to this young lady must be said without witnesses.

SNAP (*crosses to* C.).   Then all I've got to do is to exit centre, and leave you together.

NIS. (*innocently*).   No, no; that won't help us.   Even if he goes (*crossing to* C.) we may be interrupted.   Papa may come in any moment.

SNAP.   She thinks of everything, just like my wife.

NIS. (*to* JACK).   I don't suppose you could write to me?

JACK (*eagerly*).   No; that's quite impossible.

SNAP (*wickedly*).   Quite impossible.   There are some things that can only be settled by one's own lips.

[NISBE *crosses*, R., *in a huff.*

[*READY* PROFESSOR, *with valise half full, to enter* L. D.

JACK.   Of course I

NIS. (*naïvely*).   It's a dreadful plight, isn't it?   And I'm sorry I can't help you out.   I have to go and pack up now in there.   (*Points* R.)   This valise.   (*Goes towards* R. *with valise, and turns.*)   Is there anything so fatiguing as to have to pack a big valise all by yourself?

JACK (*goes to her eagerly*).   If you would allow me to help you —

NIS.   I should be delighted.   You know it's ever so much easier to put in things while somebody holds the valise open for you.

JACK (*takes the bag, and presses it to his heart*).   Let hold it.   I'll do it with all my heart.

NIS. (*crosses to* SNAP). I hope you will excuse us, Mr. Snap, but you see we haven't a moment to lose.

JACK (*crosses to* C.). And so much to do.

SNAP. Oh, yes, I know. Well, if you lose no time, you may catch the train.

NIS. That's so — come! (*EXITS*, R. D.)

JACK. Oh, yes. I'm coming. (*EXITS after her.*)

SNAP (*sighs*). Ah, I guess he won't need any prompter in the part he's playing now.

[*READY* ANGELICA *and* MRS. BABBITT, *to enter* L. C.

The PROFESSOR *ENTERS*, L. D., *in shirt sleeves, with a valise half full.*

PROFESSOR. I'm more than half full, and I haven't got quarter in yet. (*Puts valise on table*, L.)

SNAP (*stands before door*, R.). Excuse me, Professor, but you don't want anything in here ?

PROF. In there ? No, no.

SNAP. I'm glad of that. The fact is, I'm on guard, and nobody must go in here for fifteen minutes. I have an important engagement, and if you would only take my place —

PROF. (*beginning to pack*). Yes, but —

SNAP. The fact is, there are two people in there who are preparing a surprise for you. (*Aside.*) I'll run over to the hotel, and send his lordship. If those two in there are firm, they may get his consent on the spot. If they can't get it, they had better know the worst at once. The Professor sha'n't have more than one tragedy on his hands at the same time. (*EXIT*, L. C.)

PROF. (*sighing*). I don't believe anything will surprise me now. (*Goes up into alcove to get some wearing-apparel, which is placed there.*)

ANGELICA *ENTERS*, L. C.; *speaks back.*

ANGELICA. Come in, mamma ; there's nobody here.

MRS. BABBITT *ENTERS.*

MRS. BABBITT.   I'm glad of it.

PROF.   My wife! (*Half draws the curtain noiselessly.*)

MRS. B.   There are certain people I prefer not to see.

ANG. (L., *soothingly*).   But, mamma, we must meet papa some time.

MRS. B.   I don't see the necessity.   Attend to me.   I have given you the keys of all the other rooms.   Keep them until your father demands them; that is, if he ever has the face to communicate with you.   You may lock up this room when we leave.   I merely wish to take my portrait out of it. (*Takes portrait off the easel*, R. H.)   It is out of place.

ANG. (*has discovered the* PROFESSOR, *and says aside to* MRS. BABBITT).   Papa is up there behind the curtain.

MRS. B. (*going on with her work, speaks the following with intentional frigidity*).   Give the picture to the servant.   Let her carry it up to the garret, and store it there with the other lumber, with its face to the wall.

PROF. (*groans, and comes forward with a coat and vest in his hand*).   O Zippy, you rend my heart!

MRS. B. (*ignoring him entirely*).   With its face to the wall.   That settles it.

PROF. (*drops on his knees*).   Zippy darling, are you going · to leave your home?

MRS. B. (*speaks to* ANGELICA, *as if entirely oblivious of the* PROFESSOR'S *presence*).   I told you before, my resolve is ir-revocable.   I shall go with my poor penitent Nisbe to my sister in Boston.   The train leaves at 12.20.   There we shall both be safe from contamination and deceit.

PROF. (R.).   Zippy, look at me.

MRS. B. (*to* ANGELICA).   Did you speak? (PROFESSOR *totters to his feet and buries himself on sofa at fire.*)

ANG. (L.).   Don't be so harsh, mamma.   I have forgiven Harry.

MRS. B. (*contemptuously*).   Indeed!

ANG.   We had an explanation, and made it all up.   To be sure, he was guilty in deceiving me; but as his deception was in trying to make me believe he was worse instead of better, I could easily forgive it.   He is a perfect angel.   He has no past.   He never had a past.   I think I like him that way best.   [*READY* MULBERRY, *to enter* L. C.

MRS. B. (L. C.).   Really!   So he's got you to believe him again?   Poor lamb!   But your husband has youth as an excuse.   He hasn't played the clown at sixty,

[PROFESSOR *groans.*

and disgraced a gray-haired wife and grown-up children. He hasn't descended to the meanness of plotting with your domestics behind your back.

PROF. (*coming down*).   But, Zippy!   I only tried to give you a pleasant surprise.

MRS. B. (*still addressing* ANGELICA).   A pleasant surprise, indeed!   You've made a fool of yourself, and all of us, before the whole town.   I could have forgiven anything but that.   (*Crosses to* R.)

PROF. (C.).   I can't argue with the back of your head! (*Goes* L., *angrily.*)   If you won't look at a person! (*Commences to pack things furiously in valise on table,* L.)

MRS. B. (*to* ANGELICA).   Now help me to pack this basket.

[*They go,* R., *to basket; and during the following* ANGELICA *opens the cabinet and helps her mother to pack silverware, small boxes, jewel-cases, etc.*

LORD MULBERRY *ENTERS,* L. C.

MULBERRY.   Here I am, dear friends.

PROF. (*testily, after looking at him*).   Oh, bother!   (*Packs valise more vehemently, pulling out two articles to put in one, etc.*)

MUL. (*looking at his watch*). The train starts in an hour, so if we make haste we can talk it all over.

MRS. B. (*aside, vexed*). What does he want now? (*Wraps up articles handed by* ANGELICA, *and packs vigorously.*)

MUL. I suppose you've been expecting me?

PROF. (L., *impatiently*). Can't say we have.

MUL. (*poking him in the side*). Capital! Oh, play the indifferent! The father of the girl always does. But of course you don't mean it. That Mr. Snap told me everything is as good as settled.

> [*The* PROFESSOR *looks at him, holds up his hands in puzzled expression, and packs.*

MRS. B. (*looks at* ANGELICA *and then at* MULBERRY). But, sir, you see we are busy.

MUL. Oh, packing! Don't let me stand in your way. Perhaps I can help you; I understand the art to perfection. (*Takes an ornament from* L. *table and wraps it in several scraps of paper which he takes from the waste-basket.*)

PROF. (*impatiently*). May I ask what you wish here, anyhow?

MUL. (*laughing*). What I wish? That's capital. That's neat. (*To others.*) Now, listen to the Professor, ladies, coolly asking me what I wish. (*Crosses to* PROFESSOR, *still wrapping the ornament.*) Why, you sly dog you, how can you play off so? You'd make a capital actor. Ladies (*crosses to them, still wrapping*), he'd make his fortune on the stage. He ought to play in that piece I saw over the way last night. [*The ladies exclaim. General groan.*

PROF. Will you, once for all —

MUL. (*nudges him*). How do you like my son, now that you know him, eh? I think him changed — changed for the better. (*Puts the ornament he was wrapping in the basket, and packs it in.*) And why? — eh? — why? (*Nudges him.*) It's love. (*Picks up another article from the table,* L.

and commences to wrap it up in newspaper, which he takes from table.) " Oh, 'tis love, 'tis love ! " etc.

PROF. (L., *in despair*). Possibly. Anything you like —

MUL. (*to* MRS. BABBITT). Madame, he'll make the best husband in the world ! (*Packs the last article he has been wrapping in her basket.*) The boy is so good-hearted ! (*Takes a bead cushion from an armchair near by, and begins to wrap that up.*) You have no idea how much he esteems and values your whole family. (*About to put the cushion in the basket.*)

MRS. B. (*preventing him*). What are you doing there ?

MUL. Oh, isn't this going ? (*Pulls cushion out and throws it on sofa.*) He told me all about it last night. Confided in me. He never confided in me before — and I consented. (*Commences to wrap up a footstool which he picks from the floor.*) I know it's all right, for the rascal has excellent taste. 'Gad ! so have I ; it runs in the family. And now, as to what the young people will have to live on. (*About to pack the footstool in the* PROFESSOR'S *valise.*)

[*READY* NISBE *and* JACK, *to enter* R. D

PROF. (*hurls footstool away*). You must be aware all this doesn't interest us.

MUL. (*seizing his hand*). Noble sentiment ! But the children must live. (*Crosses to* MRS. BABBITT.) My boy is just like your husband, no thought of the morrow. He takes the girl just as she is, but you and I are sensible.

[*READY* DAMASK, *to enter* L. C.

MRS. B. (*sarcastically*). I have strong doubts. (*To* PROFESSOR.) How long is this to last ? Mr. Babbitt, will you quietly but firmly show this person the door ?

MUL. (*amazed*). Show me the door ! But I thought it was all right. My son led me to believe — and that Mr. Snap assured me ! Why, I thought that you and I should dance together at the wedding.

MRS. B. (R.). In the name of all that's irritating, at lose wedding ?

NISBE *and* JACK *ENTER*, R. *door, hand in hand.*

JACK. At ours, I hope! (*To* MULBERRY, *presenting* NISBE.) Well, sir, did I exaggerate? Here is your daughter.

MRS. B. What's this? Nisbe! Mr. Babbitt!

PROF. This is the surprise Snap spoke of.

NISBE (*crosses to him*). I couldn't help it, papa. Mr. Cassius made love so naturally.

MUL. (*joining their hands*). You see, I was right after all. [MRS. BABBITT *and* PROFESSOR *go* L. *for explanations.*

DAMASK *ENTERS*, L. C.

DAMASK. Professor, great news!

ANG. What is it?

PROF. Never mind your news. We've got the greatest news in here just now.

DAM. Oh, I see! (*Crosses to* ANGELICA; *shakes hands with* JACK.) I congratulate you. (*To all.*) But that's a minor consideration. Only think, I've been told all over the city that the performance last night ended in a great success after all.

ANG.		What?
MRS. B.	(*together*).	Is it possible!
NIS. (*hugging him*).		O papa!
PROF.		I don't want to hear another word about it.

MUL. Do you refer to the play over the way at the Opera House last night?   [*READY* SNAP, *to enter* L. C.

DAM. Of course.

MUL. I was there.

MRS. B., DAM., *and* ANG. Well?

PROF. (*crosses to him*). Well, how was it?

MUL. A great success! Capital piece! I never saw anything finer.

DAM. I told you!

NIS. *and* ANG. ⎞
MRS. B.   ⎠ (*together*). There, papa! Justinian!

[*READY* SUSAN, *with basket, to enter* L. C.

PROF. But I thought the curtain had to be dropped in the middle of the second act.

MUL. So I heard. I did not arrive till later. I was told there had been some interruption.

DAM. But the management skilfully turned the tide of feeling, and the performance went on to a happy conclusion.

PROF. (*rubbing his hands*). So they liked it?

MUL. Immensely.

MRS. B. Justinian, this atones for everything!

SNAP *ENTERS, hastily,* L. C.

SNAP. Professor! Professor! Have you heard? We had a gigantic success after all, last night.

MRS. B. (*crosses to him*). Yes, we've heard all! (*Offers her hand.*) And I forgive you for the uncle and Camille.

PROF. Now we'll all take a holiday together. Suppose, instead of taking it in different directions, we all go to New York?

MUL. With me? That will be delightful.

PROF. Let's pack, then; we've only forty minutes.

ALL (*in commotion*). We'll all help!

SUSAN *ENTERS,* L. C., *with clothes-basket nearly full of knick-knacks. And from now until curtain falls all busy themselves with packing.* MRS. BABBITT *down* R. *with* ANGELICA. DAMASK *and* JACK *with* NISBE, L. PROFESSOR *and* SNAP *down* C. MULBERRY *and* SUSAN *running with articles between each group.*

SNAP (*to* PROFESSOR, *aside*). Don't come back too soon.

PROF.   What do you mean?

SNAP.   The performance last night was saved by my wife's presence of mind again.

PROF.   She's a trump!

SNAP.   She is.   When she saw that your piece was irretrievably damned (*all stop packing*) in the second act —

PROF.   Well, well?

SNAP.   She dropped your tragedy altogether, and substituted in its place —

PROF.   What?   [*READY curtain*

SNAP.   A NIGHT OFF!!!

> [PROFESSOR *sinks in chair. Amid the animation and confusion of packing, and just as* JACK *is kissing* NISBE, *the*

CURTAIN FALLS.

FARCES

TANGLES

Farce in One Act. Four Males, Two Females

By C. Leona Dalrymple

One interior scene. Bill Tracy accepts Mrs. Janeway's invitation to dinner, intended for his cousin, Phil. Tracy, who is Jack Janeway's chum. Elsie, her maid, advertised for a husband under the soubriquet of "Bright Eyes." Jenkins, Bill's valet, answers it as X. Y. Z. The mistakes in identity get them into a tangle of surprises, finally unraveled by Jack, who arrives opportunely. The "situations" are tremendously funny and keep the audience in roars of laughter. Plays forty-five minutes.

PRICE 15 CENTS

A NIGHT IN TAPPAN

Farce in One Act. Two Males, Three Females

By O. B. Dubois

One interior scene. The action commences at 10:45 P. M., on th arrival of Mr. and Mrs. John Betts, quite unexpectedly, at the home of Mr. Augustus Betts, while Mrs. Augustus Betts is awaiting her husband's return from the city. The complications caused by a saucy, blundering, Irish servant, Mr. Augustus being entirely ignorant of the new arrivals, are screamingly bewildering. Plays about thirty minutes.

PRICE 15 CENTS

KISSING THE WRONG GIRL

Farce in One Act. One Male, Two Females

By W. C. Parker

No scenery needed. It is the case of a "cheeky" book-agent, two sisters who look much alike, all sorts of funny mistakes, and any number of ridiculous situations, that will keep the audience in a continuous roar of laughter. The piece can be played either "straight" or with specialties. Plays about thirty minutes.

PRICE 15 CENTS

THE NEW REPORTER

Farce in One Act. Six Males, Two Females

By Franklin Johnston

One interior scene. Hobbs, the proprietor of a newspaper, is expecting a new reporter, whom he has engaged on trial. Nancy, Hobbs' daughter, persuades her lover, Jack, who is unknown to her father, to personify the new reporter, and gets to work. The blunders he makes, and the arrival of Tupper, the real reporter, result in a general flare-up, until explanations are made, and Tupper is persuaded by Nancy to retire in favor of Jack. Plays forty-five minutes.

PRICE 15 CENTS

MA'S NEW BOARDERS

Farce in One Act. Four Males, Four Females

By W. C. Parker

No scenery required. Mrs. Holdtight leaves her boarding-house in her daughter's charge. Prof. Alto-Gether calls a rehearsal of the village choir, but gives them the wrong address. The choir turns u at Mrs. H.'s, and are mistaken for new boarders. Then follows a uproarious series of incidents that end in the Professor's round-up. Can be played "straight" or with specialties. Excellent chance for single or double quartette. Plays thirty minutes.

PRICE 15 CENTS

Lightning Source UK Ltd.
Milton Keynes UK
UKHW021826060119
335045UK00012B/1256/P

RUNECASTER

~RUNECASTER~

AN OTHERWORLD ANTHOLOGY

BY

V. S. ARMSTRONG.

INCLUDING AN INTRODUCTION

BY

RUMPELSTILTSKIN.

1

RUNECASTER

First printed in the European Economic Community in 2001.

First published in the European Economic Community in 2001.

Published by V. S. Armstrong.

ISBN: 1-904032-00-1

RUNECASTER

~TO RAPUNZEL~

"Rapunzel, Rapunzel, who can she be?
It could be you or maybe me,
Yet, of one thing we can be sure:
Her heart of gold is warm and pure.

Unto yourself you must be true,
Especially if your eyes are blue,
And if you crave for Celtic spells,
You'll find them in the Book of Kells."

RUNECASTER

~ACKNOWLEDGEMENTS~

'An introduction to Celtic Mythology' by David Bellingham has proved essential to the researching of this subject.

The mythological paintings of Jim Fitzpatrick in books such as 'Erin Saga' provide an important source of inspiration to me as a writer.

The poems in this book, attributed to fictitious characters or factual characters or without attribution are all written by the author.

RUNECASTER

~LOREMASTER~

"Bitter is this heart of mine,
For whom words resound with rhyme,
And for whom each verse I've wrote,
Ends up sounding like a quote.

Gleaning gold from threshing straw,
Fills the mortal heart with awe,
Yet, I would a simpler spell,
If I had a tale to tell."

Rumpelstiltskin.

5

RUNECASTER

~AN TÓR GLOINE~

Once, in legend long ago,
On a strange and distant shore,
Dwelt a dire and darksome foe,
Balor, of the fell Fomor.

Ethne, fair and unsurpassed,
On the shores of Hy-Brasyl,
Fettered was her heart's repast,
Bound unto her father's will.

Chaste, the tears that she did cry,
As to sorrow, she was prone,
Escaped her lips, a wistful sigh,
Virtue's doom, to dwell alone.

"An Tór Gloine", her domain,
Lest a stranger, her espy,
Sorrowful her triste refrain,
'Neath the withered evil eye.

Imprisoned thus, by dire decree,
Eager dreams anticipate,
She, no man might ever see,
Tower of Glass, her destined fate.

RUNECASTER

~AOIFE~

Their mother sadly passed away,
Ere Aoife came to stay,
She slept alone beneath the earth,
Whilst minstrels played her praises worth,
Yet, Aoife eased Lear's broken heart,
As thus her sister did depart,
Upon that fateful day.

"How I remember as a child,
Running wild, running free;
To feel the rain upon your back,
Need no imagination lack:
Swift lay thy garb upon the frond,
The lake as shallow as a pond,"
Her voice in manner mild.

Each hastened, Aoife to obey,
Despite her face so wan,
Who cloaked in darkness spread her arms,
To conjure her transforming charms:
Four children she laid curse upon,
Turned each into a winsome swan,
And sadly flew away.

RUNECASTER

~ARIADWEN~

"Ariadwen, spindle sprite,
Patience is thy heart's delight,
Spinning strands of wondrous web,
As the tides, they flow and ebb.

Finally, the spiral spun,
With the setting of each sun,
Gossamer aglow, the gloaming,
As within my thoughts a roaming.

Passing patiently, the eve,
She, in darkness shall deceive,
Dew drops on her web may glisten,
Silently, she stops to listen.

Though the winds, her web may loose,
She inspires the noble Bruce,
Right resolved to make repair,
Never time to feel despair.

If at first you don't succeed,
Virtue true may intercede,
For, a kingdom may seem lost,
If conceit was all it cost."

RUNECASTER

~ASPENVAR~

"The moon beams bright mid darkling dell,
Upon Fay, Aspenvar.
Will-o'-the-wisp, thou sibling sprite,
Cloaked 'neath enchantment of the night.
And soft, the starlight in her hair,
Meek mortal dreams shall thus ensnare,
Beneath her darksome spell.

Lo! Aspenvar, such mortal guise,
Is this thy chosen doom?
Forsaken, thine immortal span,
Who would be wed to mortal man,
In whom death knows such foolish fear?
~To live a day and half a year,
In thine adoring eyes!

Dark Aspenvar, dreams dissipate,
Reseda is thine E'lven gaze,
Concealing tristful, tearful haze.
~I care not for the passing hours,
Our love is set amongst the stars,
Whose silent soul may ne'er implore,
To see that banished Valar shore!"

From the Annals of Aspenvar.

RUNECASTER

~AVALON~

"As bleary eyed, my senses blur,
Time, out of reason, doeth concur,
That words are brush strokes of the art,
Which from my dreams these scrawls impart:
A rainbow in a summer sky,
With which my surging senses vie,
To capture waves in ecstasy,
Within commotions of the sea.
Whilst fleeting birds soar there on high,
Awash with colour, seasons fly,
Now, as I seek that thousandth word,
My foolish thoughts may seem absurd.
Yet, there upon the verbal beach,
Lie synonyms within my reach:
These jaded waves upon the shore,
Do daubs of thriving foam implore,
And might not foliated trees,
Catch splendour from the sun with ease?
Reflected forms of penury,
Shall thrive within this estuary:
A dappled duck impatient pleads:
"My drake hides nigh within those reeds."
And as these weirding words I will,
With scratching of my feathered quill,
The magic of a Fairie glen,
Shall thrill anon my hopes again:
Proud pageant there before mine eyes,
Doeth thus enthrall with Elven guise.
From rhyming pallet, shall I glean,
The babbling of a rushing stream:
Where Dryads dipped their rooted rhymes,
Within the ink of favoured times.
And here within this phras'ed theme,
Apt adjectives shall thus redeem,
Fay fables of lost history,
When life was but a mystery..."

10

RUNECASTER

~BARROW WIGHTS~

"The weirding wights of mounded downs,
Bemoan the moonless night,
Their faces set in howling frowns,
Grave robbers to affright."

RUNECASTER

~BELTAINE~

"Fires of passion, bon fires burn,
Whilst fair maidens, yielding, yearn,
To be loved, as they would love:
'Tis the season of the dove.

Knightly errants, they can wait,
As our hearts anticipate,
Proud procession, noble fare,
Venturing to who knows where:

Gone a Maying, one and all,
As glad eyes, the Shí enthrall.
Of aught we've seen we naught must say,
Lest golden wishes fade away."

RUNECASTER

~BERENGARIA~

"Oh Berengaria, my love!
Thy tresses of Venetian red,
Beguile the heavens up above,
Whom thine angelic eyes beheld."

RUNECASTER

~BETRAYAL~

"Abide within these walls a while,
I urgently implore,
And see anon a gentle smile,
My peerless paramour.

Such love I give,
Lest hope should fail,
And I not live,
To tell the tale,

Of dolorous dolour..."

RUNECASTER

~BRANWEN~

Strewn with stars, the lunar nocturne,
As desires, within her heart burn,
To be free of mortal strife,
Whom duty bound to be a wife.

Great the sorrow, her befell,
Beneath the wrath of husband fell:
Upon her brow, heaped he such scorn,
Branwen did wish she were never born!

Her destiny, distorted dreams;
In sullen silence, muted screams:
A song thrush did she patient tame,
To speak anon of all her shame.

It flew to Wales across the sea,
To where her kin drew presently,
Bendigeidfran beckoned the bird,
Which fluttered hence without a word:

Alighting lightly upon his shoulder,
The bird grew ever more the bolder,
And at Caer Seint in fair Arfon,
The bird did sing a sombre song:

"Oh, men of Wales, heed now my plea,
For I an emissary be,
Proud Branwen bade me speak to thee,
Of all her shame and misery."

"What wonder this!" did all men cry,
For what they heard could none deny.
With urgent clamour hearts implore,
To Ireland sail and hence to war!

RUNECASTER

~BRIER ROSE~

"Were ever lips so sweet as she,
Or countenance the more carefree,
Whose tresses are the source of prose,
Thy fair and lovely Brier Rose."

RUNECASTER

~CHALUZ~

"Across the plains, nine riders rode,
As swift as flies the sparrow,
And dashed towards that dark abode,
Whence hastened hence an arrow.

Though sped the heralds after him,
Our king was all the bolder.
Thus, tempted by ill fated whim,
The barbed point pierced his shoulder.

Then stared the Lion-heart aghast,
'Pon grey goose feathered flight,
Yet, as he dared to pluck the shaft,
Dulled senses turned to night."

RUNECASTER

~CHANGELING~

"A tiny little squeal,
Of stark surprise,
As his hefty hands,
They clasped over her eyes.

Who could it be?
She could not see!
Was it a werewolf,
In gremlin guise?"

RUNECASTER

~CLONTARF~

"Proud king of old, embattled bold,
Held he aloft caduceus gold,
A cruciform authority,
Winged herald's wand of sanctity.

Age tarnished seems the High King's clasp,
Yet, victory's within our grasp,
And though our hearts be broke with woe,
Now vanquished is the Fomor foe!

Boru is slain, so it is said,
No High King more to take his stead,
And as this land may ruler lack,
The kingdom shall begin to crack."

RUNECASTER

~DEIRDRE OF THE SORROWS~

"Deirdre heard the voice of her loved one,
'Twas whistling upon the breeze.
And hastened after the setting sun,
For her heart was ill at ease.

An augury of portents,
Which bode naught else but ill,
Much agonised her torments,
And sapped her strength of will."

RUNECASTER

~DOLMEN~

"Amid the hazy heather,
Where thrives the Fairie thorn,
Stands triadelphous terror,
Askance eyes gaze upon:

Shadowed dolmen wrought of dreams,
Men raised there long ago,
A scriptorium of screams,
To pagan tales of woe."

RUNECASTER

~DRAGONSPELL~

"Oh beauteous beast, within thee hies,
A tempestuous tumult of lurid lies,
Which bid the beholder dare to dream,
Of gallant deeds as yet unseen.

Yet, should I linger here a while,
Thy lustre shall my thoughts beguile,
Until I have no will to leave,
Who fail thy cunning to perceive."

RUNECASTER

~DREAMREIVER~

"Whilst halls of Tara soft resound,
To dulcet tones of musing harp,
Knoll Navan burns unto the ground;
Endarkened timbers, wilted, warp.

Four thrones of splendour do I see,
Upon a hillside grassy green,
And death, the High King's destiny,
Our future now must seem obscene.

Yet, now the muted music vies,
From somewhere deep beneath the ground,
To send hopes soaring to the skies,
Where fleeting dragons may be found.

And still the lilt of laughter sounds,
Whilst merriment was had by all;
Here Celtic legend oft abounds:
I must concede to feeling small."

RUNECASTER

~ELIDOR~

"Reflected thoughts of clouded dreams,
Laze lacustrine in tidal themes,
Where ebb and flow the season's scorn,
Beneath the glow of Summer morn.

Know well one day, I shall return,
Unto that land dark doubts would spurn,
Or ever after rue the day,
That I did ever pass this way."

24

RUNECASTER

~ENCHANTMENT~

"Diaphanous rain fell in glistening torrents,
Amid the sultry woodland haze,
An ethereal curtain of cascading moments,
Within my languid, enchanted gaze."

RUNECASTER

~ETAIN~

"A filigree of golden curls,
About her shoulders soft unfurls,
Where raucous rush of waterfall,
Her sibling senses doeth enthrall.

And as with reason, beauty vie,
Her vivid visage, I espy,
She gently steals my wits away,
This lithesome lass, enthralling fay."

RUNECASTER

~HARBINGER~

Oh woe to the world,
That it should come to this,
The Harlander emergent in our midst,
Harbinger of Evil,
For verily it is written:

"...And he shall wield his words,
Brandishing his faith ever before him,
As a sword burnished bright,
With gifted tongues of righteous flame:
Talisman against the unholy."

Charlemagne.

RUNECASTER

~HY-BRASYL~

"Clouds melt into the sultry skies,
And gently slip away,
Where lofty Elven towers rise,
To greet the light of day."

~IGRAINE~

"She was the wife of Gorlois,
Yet Uther coveted Igraine,
And took her unto him,
And the face of the Moon,
Was sorrowed by this event,
But the light of the Sun shone,
Upon their union in blessing,
For all life is sacred."

Merlin.

RUNECASTER

~ISOBELLE~

"Gazing upon the crystalline abyss,
That lay beyond her sapphire eyes,
He felt the cold chill of her kiss,
That cruel death could not disguise.

Amid the anguish of his soul,
He wept alone, aloud in vain.
For hers were empty eyes,
Crying out in silent pain.

He clasped her soulless shell,
To brush aside her lifeless hair,
To look 'pon fair Isobelle,
Bereft of all her earthly care.

Departed was her voice of love,
Sifting slowly from his mind,
Sweet as an angel from above,
To leave this mannequin behind.

He raged against his fate,
That he remained alone,
As his anger turned to hate,
For no sins did she atone.

Conspiracy of death,
Had stole her heart away.
Thus, he remained bereft,
And cursed the light of day."

RUNECASTER

"How fast can the dragon fly,
Across a cloudless sky?
How swift doeth the unicorn,
Traverse a Summer morn.
All this and more,
Doeth thought implore,
Of life's great mystery.

For I have seen things,
No man should see,
Dreamt dreams,
Which cannot be,
Of battles bold,
And tales untold,
Beyond the farthest sea."

RUNECASTER

~LEPRECHAUN~

A fat and ugly little Troll,
With beady eyes and cheerful grin,
Sat huddled in a squatting ball,
And, pensive, preened his bearded chin.

A Fairie found him all alone,
And asked him kindly, passing by:
"Why sit you there, have you no home?"
To which the creature made reply:

"Beneath the stars, I nightly dwell,
And rest my bones against a tree;
Fresh moss for comfort serves as well,
As feathered down of majesty."

RUNECASTER

~LINDENVAR~

"The sun shone bright, that autumn dawn,
Upon fair Lindenvar.
The air was crisp and fresh with frost,
And she, within her thoughts, was lost.
As dew drops kissed her flaxen hair,
So she remained without a care,
And sang her tristful song.

Oh Lindenvar, sweet gentle maid,
Why is Love's saga sad?
Whose honey voice so charms the birds,
That stay, they dare, to hear thy words,
And dwell with thee and know no fear,
Yet shed thine eyes a sullen tear,
For one whom fate betrayed!

Dear Lindenvar, fair Elven maid,
Speak of the secret in thy heart,
That bade thus reason to depart!
~I hear the waterfall's swift dance,
Glimpsed mid the golden sun-light's gleam,
Enchanted depths of jade enhance,
This timeless world where lovers dream."

From the Legend of Lindenvar.

RUNECASTER

~MID-WINTER'S EVE~

"Beyond the sparkling ocean floe,
Doeth glimmer bright the drifting snow,
Wherein resides the Ice Princess,
Whose harrowed heart craves tenderness.

Frosting forbearance of her smile,
Shall soft, unwily wits beguile,
Mid sylvan splendour, thawing throne,
There tender we conversant tone.

Enchanted icicles on high,
Soar upwards to the searing sky,
As 'neath her piercing arctic gaze,
I humbly kneel and sing her praise."

~MOON SHADOW~

"The opal moon spread leprous light,
Upon the silent vale.
No creature stirred, yet shadows lurked,
Where foul mists broiled the sultry earth,
And nameless spectres dwell.

What is this sorry silhouette,
That I espy nearby?
A shadow soul mine eyes beget,
As terror doeth my heart beset,
And with wrought reason vie."

From the Ballad of Uther and Igraine.

RUNECASTER

~MORSINE~

"Proud queen of Celts,
The fey Morsine,
Garbed in fur pelts,
Gemmed throne serene:

Perceived the souls,
Of suitor's guile,
And bade the fools,
To rest a while."

RUNECASTER

~MOY TURA~

"They clashed so bravely,
As their armies took the field:
Foes battling courageously,
For no quarter would they yield.

So mighty was the shock,
Heroes gathered to the throng,
Knowing shields would interlock,
In the legend of new song."

RUNECASTER

~NOCTURNE~

"Sparkling spritely, gleaming glitter,
Seasoned nightly, frost may fritter,
Away all cares of toil and worth,
Betwixt the stars of heaven's girth."

RUNECASTER

~NORSEMEN~

" 'Twas in the merry month of May,
My true love browsed upon the beach,
When Viking longships sailed this way,
And found her here within their reach.

Alas! Alack! To her dismay,
They held her fast with grim resolve,
And as her hopes did fade away,
Romantic dreams too swift dissolve.

No reprieve was there to her plight,
For all had fled towards the tower,
At dusk they slipped into the night,
I would this were my final hour!"

RUNECASTER

~NIGHTMARE~

"With frosting breath and eyes aflame,
Out of the night the shadow came:
Upon a dire, dark night-mare steed,
From the foul realms of the undead,
Whose darkling rider bore the horns,
Of a fell stag upon his head."

From the Legend of Hearn the Hunter.

RUNECASTER

~NIMUE~

"The alembic of fancy;
Liquefaction of thought,
Brighten eyes I deem dancy,
As my gaze, they have caught:

In the wonder of dreams,
As I wish she were mine,
How their beauty now seems,
To be less than divine:

For those lips, I would kiss,
In the wink of a trice,
And partake of such bliss,
Were her fate not the price."

Merlin.

RUNECASTER

~ODE TO AFFRECA~

"I tarry here alone,
In this prison of my soul:
So far away from home,
That this Time, I can not thole.

For my irksome body strives,
Though the journey seems so long,
To reunite our lives,
And craves the rhythm of thy song.

Thus, I hasten in my dream,
For my spirit begs be free:
As a glistening, prancing stream,
Downward rushing to the sea:

And my fantasies contrive,
That I may steal myself to thee;
For with thee I am alive:
Such love thine eyes invest in me."

Sir John de Courcy.

44

RUNECASTER

~ODE TO TITANIA~

"The time of magic is at hand,
Within this sphere of revelry,
When all that glisters in this land,
Shall set the whim of fancy free.

Titania, midst thy Fairie throng:
Whilst time and seasons emanate,
The night is young, and Love so strong,
Ere passion's verve doeth dissipate.

The gloaming shall bedew thine eyes,
A nectar of nocturnal prose,
Purview to all that lids apprise,
On which deep dreams of night impose,

A grammar of enchanted thyme,
Instilling thoughts of emptiness;
Sedulity of clouds sublime:
Fond fragrance to Love's tenderness.

Filch from thine eyes proud reason's taint,
For bawdy dreams shall come to pass,
And with lewd lust thy heart acquaint,
Whilst thus enamoured of an ass."

Oberon.

RUNECASTER

~PHANTASM~

"What fateful chance that she should stray,
As daylight softly fades away,
Unto the Forest of the Weir,
Her thoughts, foreboding filled with fear.

Nor would she live to tell the tale,
Of pallid phantoms deathly pale,
Where creatures of the night abound,
Lo, heavenly angels to confound.

There rests the Chalice of moot lore,
That men have sought and lost before:
Where taunt of visions, hopes to pale,
Mock those who sought the Holy Grail."

RUNECASTER

~REFLECTIONS~

"Within the lacustrine allure,
Of woodland waters, still and pure,
Beyond the mirrored surface lie,
Reflected depths in my mind's eye:
~Another world unseen.

There spritely visions I espy,
Of distant realms where pixies vie,
With colocynth and celandine;
And briar rose of eglantine:
~For favours of their queen.

Titania in her ivy bower,
To mark the waxing of each hour,
Shall from a nimble acorn cup,
Dreams, nectar laden, gently sup:
~With Elven lips serene.

'Neath petal lids of pallid hue,
She sees aught that her subjects do,
Bright eyes alighting soft upon,
Her lord and master, Oberon:
~Who holds her in esteem.

As she within enchantment dwells,
Surrounded by the Dryad dells,
Dew laden gleams her mantle royal,
A gossamer gown of Satyr toil,
~In Love's recurring theme.

The vision fades, her heart wanes dim,
Whilst cloudy shades of night draw in,
As gently are the stars unfurled,
Within this fleeting Otherworld:
~Too seldom we have seen."

RUNECASTER

~ROWANVAR~

"Whilst thou art captive in my arms,
My pallid Rowanvar:
The terebinthine scented air,
Thoughts fragrance laden debonair,
Belie the stars that shine so bright,
Which gird the forest of the night,
For Time itself stood still.

Oh Rowanvar, mine Elven love,
Though downcast be thine eyes:
In marody of dark desires,
Pulse perfidy of passion's fires,
Terse testament to forlorn fear,
Lest disenchantment of a tear,
Besmirch thy fallow fare!

Autumnal temptress, Rowanvar,
The tithe of time, my thoughts incline.
Towards the love two hearts entwine:
~I would that I might pass a day,
Whence merry Elven minstrels play,
And jig with spritely maidens fair,
Where mortals know no earthly care."

From the Treatise of Rowanvar.

48

RUNECASTER

~RUNECASTER~

"Fantasy, the Foreboding!
The taunt of Time,
In weirding rhyme:
Shall render aught but sooth sublime.

Mellow, the Murmuring!
Seer of sorrow,
Bind the morrow,
With this blood of life we borrow.

Omen, the unholy!
Dire deeds disrupt,
And action prompt,
Abomination, gods affront.

Prophesy, the Foretelling!
The hand of fate,
We anticipate,
As chanting terrors dissipate."

RUNECASTER

~RUNE STONE~

"Eyes, crystalline composure mid the frosted frore,
Trace firming furrows we have paced before,
Where, blunt athwart the stark rune stone,
Whip winds that rip raw to the bone.

Time's swirling eddies ripple there,
Where wend the echoes of no-where,
And bind the dead unto their oath,
Who rouse from slumber, limbs of sloth.

Wraiths gather round ligneous stone:
Faithbreakers, who must now atone,
Though cracked, cursed bones of seeping marrow,
They animate eyes pierced with arrow.

Hence slouch they onward in a dream,
As silence from their wailings scream,
Whilst raised curled trumpets wrought of horn,
To chastened lips of grimaced scorn.

Yet, even now men tell the story,
Of how wroth wraiths redeemed their glory,
And rose upon the fated hour,
With rusted blades and faces dour."

RUNECASTER

~SACRIFICE~

"Within the misted moon's repose,
Lurk restless spirits we depose,
As 'twixt the windward rushing reeds,
A howling, vacant voice recedes.

Into the distance of our soul,
With weirdings we can never thole,
Cry spirits of the dire undead,
Whose reason yet may turn our head.

Is that the rustling of the leaves?
Such ventures do our thoughts deceive.
And is that shadow near at hand,
Now closer to this face so bland?

As blanched be reason from our eyes,
Whose countenance doeth fear disguise,
I would I never went this way,
Where banished seems the light of day.

Eternal is this deathly night,
Just cause for souls to take affright,
For fog of sins shall make amends,
Whose hearts the reaping reiver rends.

And as I sink into the mire,
Whilst bound constrained by forces dire,
We silence keep within our plight,
Who die alone this fateful night:

Lest spectres nigh should take offence,
And force from us such recompense,
As would give angels o'er to weeping,
Who view us 'neath this stench slide seeping..."

RUNECASTER

~SETANTA~

"Cú Chulainn, in his battle rage,
Could only Morrigu assuage,
Since none his ardour might surpass,
Though failing was his strength at last.

Bound he himself unto a stone,
Who would not deign his fate bemoan:
Proud, there he stood whom death deny,
Until was heard the Raven's cry.

For of his foes not one was bolder,
Than he alighting on his shoulder,
To gaze upon the multitude,
Who hid their shame beneath doubt's hood."

RUNECASTER

~SIONNA~

"Winsome as a wand,
Slender as a shadow,
Midst the fairie frond,
Mellow as a meadow.

Cunning as a fox,
Elusive as a lark,
Betwixt her russet locks,
Her eyes, my thoughts endark."

RUNECASTER

~STARGAZER~

"Once upon a time,
Or so the story goes,
There lived a palatine,
Whose heart was filled with prose.

Many were the waking hours,
He would pass the nights away;
In contemplation of the stars:
To where his fancies, they did stray.

Thus, as morning light did break,
Would he take himself abed,
And whilst others were awake,
So he snored asleep instead!"

From the Ballad of King Lear

RUNECASTER

~STONEHENGE~

"On Salisbury plain, at stark Stonehenge,
Druidic rites in this fair land,
Whilst heedless to the gods' revenge,
Were outlawed at the King's command.

For in this stoic Christian realm,
Before the pagan fool had fled,
Cold moonlight glinted on a helm,
As horsemen made to hack his head.

And as his neck was bloody hewn,
They cursed the druid, arrant nave.
Upon the ground, his bones lay strewn,
Men made for him a shallow grave.

Yet, to this day his cries are heard,
Beneath the fullness of the moon.
For bards of old his faith have shared:
The Dark is rising all too soon!"

From the Chronicles of King Constantine.

RUNECASTER

~TEREBINTHIA~

"The terebinthine frosted frore,
May 'neath our feet glisten encore,
As Winter, setting on a pace,
Shall cause young hearts to gladly race.

They frolic in the firmament,
Of snow-flakes that seem heaven sent:
For whilst the sibling Snow Queen reign,
You never shall find two the same."

RUNECASTER

~THE BAYEUX TAPESTRY~

"Word of invasion reached the king,
Whilst southward he was sallying,
Forth from the fray at Stamford Bridge,
To hold the fort on Hastings' Ridge.

The House Karls waded in with axe,
And dealt the Normans mighty whacks.
'Twas then Duke William turned in feint,
Whilst, heedless to their king's complaint,

The Saxons hastened down the hill,
Who could of battle have no fill:
And thus the deadly trap was sprung.
King Harold then his clenched fists wrung.

Yet, ere defeat he did espy,
An arrow took him in the eye.
Now, as the vanquished king lies dead,
Commend we valiant deeds to thread."

RUNECASTER

~THE CELTS~

"We, an ancient people are,
Journeyed hence from lands afar:
Mortal glory is our story,
Steeped in deeds both brave and dour."

RUNECASTER

~THE CHILDREN OF LEAR~

Amid the languid, leafy glade,
I strode alone, no sound I made.
For there within the weirding wood,
A spectral figure calmly stood.

An ermine mantle, Elven green,
Clad o'er her shoulders, soft serene.
She bade me hearken, passing by,
Unto her wailing ghostly cry.

Her pointing finger did implore:
"Forsaken though, the tales of yore,
Know there upon that lonesome shore,
Where Longships venture never more,

Surcease of sorrow, Suzerain!
Shall venture to these shores again,
As swanning siblings of the night,
Lear's children, downing feathers dight."

RUNECASTER

~THE CROW~

"Athwart the gnarled and twisted stem,
Of leafless twigs in requiem,
A gawking crow calmly displayed,
A rueful woe as branches swayed.

In flighted thaw, conspicuous caw,
He glides betwixt the tangled trees,
Where Winter's maw may cause us awe,
In superstition, ill at ease.

Was it not he who gleams with glee,
Queen Maeve did send on errands dire,
In lands of Shí where spirits flee,
As smoulders thus the battle pyre?"

RUNECASTER

~THE DRAGON~

"Draco gazed upon the inauspicious stars,
And sensed his destined fate.
The regret of some mere solitary hours,
Could never expiate.

For Karlin, in his heart was stout,
Though sly Draco was cunning and clever.
So in bold challenge did he shout,
To where the beast sprawled upon his treasure.

God's wrath, would he surpass,
The heart of time itself stood still,
The shattered hour glass,
A warrior has come to kill!

So Draco, battle waged,
His death his finest hour.
Slain by a deadly blade,
Forged from a fallen star."

RUNECASTER

~THE FIELD OF VALOUR~

"A broken land,
A sundered realm.
Lost crown of Counts,
The Golden Helm.

His sword now lies shattered,
With a fair Lady's token.
On his languorous lips,
Linger words yet unspoken;

Whimsical platitudes,
He had saved for the morrow:
His two leaden eyes,
Are now burdened with sorrow.

Now life is departed,
Along with his pride,
This one who did battle,
And so nobly died."

RUNECASTER

~THE FLANDERS MAID~

"As I was roving out, one morn,
A maid did I espy:
Her eyes were laden with such scorn,
As I was passing by.

Yet, how I would that she were mine,
To love and call mine own.
Whose torrid tresses flow divine,
Should warm kith, hearth and home."

~THE GOLDEN BOWER~

"Four noble Queens of Avalon,
'Twixt forest auriferous fair,
Perchanced one day to stray upon,
Sir Lancelot, who slumbered where:

The golden bower beckons,
Softly strewn with desultory dreams,
Of fragrant effervescence,
Flowing forth, amidst molten beams."

RUNECASTER

~THE LADY OF SHALLOT~

"The counterfeit of thine affections,
I do thus decry,
For wouldst thou have me live reflections,
Of a sordid lie!

Yet, I am wed for all my shame,
Unto the russet tressed Elaine:
Whose entokened eyes of Peridot,
Shall bear the shame of fair Shallot."

Lancelot.

RUNECASTER

~THE LADY OF THE LAKE~

"Beyond the shadow of despair,
Am I forsaken out of fear.
They tarry not nor venture there.
For know death's veil is ever near.

Oh mist of night, enshroud my woe;
Conceal me from, the prying foe.
Be still my heart, allay my fear:
The enemy at hand draws near."

"Let not this darkling shroud of night,
Thee, gentle spirit, to affright,
Nor hie in haste away from me,
For I am mortal, just as thee.

Though rustling leaves upon the trees,
Do cause thee to be ill at ease.
Within her chariot of light,
The fleeting moon shines opal bright.

She heeds me not and flies away,
Shall I pursue ere light of day?
Or linger here a little while,
Perchance to glimpse her gentle smile?"

From the Ballad of Uther and Igraine.

RUNECASTER

~THE MOUNTAIN KING~

"A woodland knight of Elven green,
Whose retinue as yet unseen,
Did dance a fugue of fairie fare,
Whilst of my gaze quite unaware,

The Valar host beneath the sky,
Fain, frolic in the glades nearby.
As parted I the leaf with ease,
There wafted thence a gentle breeze.

Lo and behold, before mine eyes,
The noble Elves seemed quite surprised.
For ere a word I dared to say,
All gathered swiftly fled away.

And as alone I dared remain,
I only have myself to blame.
Yet, still the lilt of dulcet tone,
Lost days of yore, anon bemoan,

From farther off and yet not far,
Ere I, their festive seasons mar,
Renewed in vigour and delight,
To simply vanish with the night."

RUNECASTER

~THE QUEEN OF DARKNESS~

"Born out of legend long ago,
Lost is her tale of mystic woe,
Who wields enchantment with a glance,
Fixated eyes, tentative trance:

Wherein the weird of distant dreams,
Invokes the vial of mortal screams,
For magic lingers in her hands,
Who ventures here from Elven lands."

RUNECASTER

~THE ROUND TABLE~

"Lost is that lore,
From times long past,
For proud Pelinore,
Hath fought his last.

Now tales of yore,
Have passed me by,
Where dragons roar,
And gryphons fly.

Fond memories of Old,
Do dwindle with the years,
And deeds as yet untold,
Fair brim my heart with tears.

Pray, Arthur's knights,
Shall linger then,
Within the hearts,
And minds of men.

For I am but a weary soul,
To whom this fleeting life seems droll,
Yet, who am I alone to say,
That legends merely fade away."

RUNECASTER

~THE SILENT SEA~

"Beyond the edge, there lies the Silent Sea!
That eery, shimmering ocean of ice,
But who can venture there, to paradise?
None save the Shí."

RUNECASTER

~THE STANDING STONE~

"The Menhir nigh the mound,
Stands on unhallowed ground,
Where king's of sullied lore,
Faith's fealty forswore:

Who dare to darkness deign,
The span of their cruel reign;
Forsaking kith and kin,
Whom bloodshed would begin."

Mordred.

RUNECASTER

~THE STORM OF WAR~

"Though seasons balked at storm of war,
The French prepared to meet their foe.
Soon exploits would be sung in lore,
And sorrows writ in tales of woe."

From the Ballad of Bouvines.

RUNECASTER

~THE TOWER~

"In lands unfit for man nor beast,
There lies the tower, in the callous east.
Beyond the forest of despair,
Across the mire where no man dare.

The brave and foolish quest in vain,
And naught of them is seen again.
'Tis folly foul to venture there.
Beware! Beware! Beware!"

RUNECASTER

~THE WEIRDING~

"Senach, in thy darkling cowl,
That the mottled moon befoul,
Shadow spectre, demon dour,
Thee, the souls of men devour."

RUNECASTER

~THE WILDCAT~

"The wildcat's senses sharpen,
As danger nears,
She waits to see what will happen,
She waits and fears.

The enemy plummets from the skies,
Oh Horror! 'Tis the eagle!
The eagle pounces upon her thighs,
The cat begins to feel feeble.

The razor sharp talons tighten,
She cries.
The eagle eyes do her frighten.
She dies."

Merlin.

RUNECASTER

~THE WILD ROSE~

"Amidst the leaf unfurling fern,
There thrives the loganberry bush,
Lo, after which my heart doeth yearn,
To hear the singing of the thrush.

The pallid rose shines bright with dew,
As effervescent beams renew,
Impassioned perpetuity,
Of early morning eulogy."

RUNECASTER

~THE WILD WOOD~

"While not the darkling hours away,
Where dire wolves wait or pixies play,
For here within this weirding world,
That foolish thoughts have left unfurled,

There lurk the creatures of the night,
Whom mortal souls perceive with fright;
And as the hunting horn is blown,
So shall deception's seed be sown:

A flighted arrow hastens where,
The deer stoop grazing, unaware.
Thus, shall the huntsman misconstrue,
The russet of his kingly hue.

To rid us of this heathen king,
With falsehood shall all voices ring,
Who banished hence our Saint Anselm,
Archbishop whom his will condemn:

To exile in some foreign land,
By decree of his cruel command:
Whilst pagan rites, the tyrant's whim.
To death, commend his soul of sin!"

From the Ballad of William Rufus.

RUNECASTER

~TRISTRAM AND ISOLDE~

"Isolde drains the cup of life,
And thus imbibes of passion's strife,
For to Tristram she would be true,
Whose love her body doeth imbue:

With all the wonders of an age,
In which is banished wisdom's sage;
Whilst set aside all mortal care,
Whom of their fate seem unaware.

Who dare to live but for today,
Whilst careworn thoughts may drift astray,
Romantic waxes revelry,
Immortalised their destiny."

RUNECASTER

~VALHALLA~

"A lonely vigil, bye and bye,
As I within this entrance sigh,
Gentle repast,
A thankless task,
For whom was cast the fated die.

What need the dead of rune repose,
As slinking shadows softly creep,
Since I was chose,
As night did close,
To share the seance of his sleep.

In souterrain, they placed the theign,
And laid war weary bones to rest.
Yet, on the morn,
His corpse was gone,
As was his chain mail armoured vest.

What hope have I? They'll say I lie!
How may I make my recompense?
Yet, as I linger,
A bony finger,
Beckons me to follow hence..."

RUNECASTER

~VISION~

"The intricacy of the written word,
May seem to us at times absurd.
Yet, here within our fable lies,
What I have seen with mine own eyes:

A fortress nigh a verdant velt,
Where once a forlorn lady dwelt,
And gazed upon the greenery,
Of rustic rural scenery."

RUNECASTER

~VORTIGERN~

"A fool knows not the hour,
That his death may fall upon,
And so his senses cower,
Before the dawning of each morn.

Yet, those of us who see,
Know the sorrow of the soul,
When death shall set us free,
As we reach that final toll."

RUNECASTER

~TRANSLATION OF CELTIC~

"An Tór Gloine."

'The Tower of Glass.'

The name Mórrígan or Morgana means 'sea dweller'.

The name Morsine is derived from the names Mordred and Rosine. The meaning of the name is 'sea-rose'.

The most accurate translation of "Shí" is 'Fay'.

RUNECASTER

<u>~TRANSLATION OF ELVEN~</u>

"Aspenvar."

'Dryad of the Aspen tree.'

"Rowanvar."

'Dryad of the Rowan tree.'

"Lindenvar."

'Dryad of the Linden tree.'

RUNECASTER

~NOTES~

The daughter of a king, Princess Affreca was born on the Isle of Man.

Beltaine or Bealtine is the arcane festival of May day, traditionally celebrated upon the first of that month.

The poem "Isobelle" was inspired by the song of the same name sung by Björk and is included to honour a visit made by her to Ulster.

Ambushed by the Fir Lí, having been bested in battle and had all their horses slain out from under them, the Anglo-Norman knights were obliged to retreat on foot: thus 'the prison of my soul' referred to by Sir John de Courcy in 'Ode to Affreca' is of course his body armour.

King Lear is depicted as a pre-Roman king of Britain but is also apparent in Celtic folklore as Lear, especially in Ireland. However, the respective themes are considerably at variance.

The performance of Lionel Jeffries as King Pelinore in the musical film production of "Camelot" was the inspiration for the "The Round Table" poem.

Saint Anselm was banished to exile by King William Rufus in the year 1097A.D.

'Rune Stone' the poem is dedicated to J.R.R. Tolkien.

RUNECASTER

RUNECASTER

Deirdre of the Sorrows: 20.
Dire Wolves: 81.
Dolmen: 21.
Dove: 12.
Draco (the Last Dragon): 61.
Dragons: 22,23,33,61,69,73.
Drake: 10.
Dreamreiver: 23.
Druids: 55.
Dryads: 10,47,87.
Duck: 10.
Eagle: 79.
Elaine (Lady of Shallot): 65.
Elves (the Elder Races): 9,10,30,35,47,48,59,72.
Etain: 26.
Ethne: 6.
Excalibur, the sword of sorrows: 27.
Fairies: 21,34,45,53.
Fairie Thorn: 21.
Faithbreakers: 50.
Farthest Sea: 33.
Fealty: 75.
Fern: 80.
Field of Valour: 62.
Fir Lí: 88.
Flanders: 63.
Fomor: 6,19.
Forest of the Weir: 46.
Fortress: 84.
Four Queens of Avalon: 64.
Fox: 53.
France (French): 76.
Glastonbury: 28.
Golden Helm: 62.
Gorlois: 31.
Gossamer: 8,47.
Grave: 55.
Grave Robbers: 11.
Gremlin: 18.
Harbinger: 29.

RUNECASTER

Harold Godwinson, king of England: 57.
Hearn the Hunter: 42.
Helm: 55.
Heralds: 17,19.
Holy Grail (Sacred Chalice): 46.
Horn Trumpets: 50.
House Karls: 57.
Hy-Brasyl: 6,30.
Ice Princess: 36.
Igraine: 31,37,66.
Ireland: 15,88.
Isle of Man: 88.
Isobelle: 32,88.
Isolde: 82.
J.R.R. Tolkien: 88.
Karlin: 61.
King Constantine: 55.
King Lear: 54,88.
Land of the Shí: 67.
Lark: 53.
Lear: 7,59,88.
Legend: 6,23,33,35,39,42.
Leonesse: 68.
Leprechaun: 34.
Lilies of the Field: 68.
Lindenvar: 35,87.
Lionel Jeffries: 88.
Loganberry: 80.
Longships: 41,59.
Loremaster: 5.
Mab (Queen of Darkness): 72.
Magic: 45,68,69,72.
Menhir (Standing Stone): 75.
Merlin: 27,28,31,43,79.
Minstrels: 7,48.
Moon: 9,11,31,37,51,55,66.
Moon Shadow: 37.
Mordred: 75,86.
Morrigu (Celtic Battle Goddess): 52.
Morsine: 38,86.

RUNECASTER

RUNECASTER

Stargazer: 54.
Stonehenge: 55.
Tara: 23.
Terebinthia: 56.
The Battle of Hastings: 57.
The Battle of Stamford Bridge: 57.
The Bayeux Tapestry: 57.
The Book of Kells: 3.
The Celts: 58.
The Crow: 60.
The Dark: 55.
The Flanders Maid: 63.
The Harlander: 29.
Theign: 83.
The Lady of the Lake: 66.
The Maid of the Sacred Grove: 70.
The Mountain King: 71.
The Weirding: 78.
Thyme: 45.
Titania (Fairie Queen): 45,47.
Tristram: 82.
Troll: 34.
Undead: 42,51.
Unicorn: 33.
Uther: 31,37,66.
Valar: 9.
Valhalla: 83.
Vikings: 41.
Vortigern: 85.
Waterfall: 26,35,68.
Web: 8.
Werewolf: 18.
Wildcat: 79.
Wild Rose: 80.
Wild Wood: 81.
William, duke of Normandy: 57.
William Rufus: 88.
Wraiths: 50.

RUNECASTER

"Abide within these walls a while,: 14.
"A broken land,: 62.
"Across the plains, nine riders rode,: 17.
A fat and ugly little Troll,: 34.
"A filigree of golden curls,: 26.
"A fool knows not the hour,: 85.
"A lonely vigil, bye and bye,: 83.
"Amid the hazy heather,: 21.
Amid the languid leafy glade,: 59.
"Amid the leaf unfurling fern,: 80.
"And so it came to pass that in his folly,: 69.
"Ariadwen, spindle sprite,: 8.
"As bleary eyed, my senses blur,: 10.
"As I was roving out, one morn,: 63.
"Athwart the gnarled and twisted stem,: 60.
"A tiny little squeal of stark surprise,: 18.
"A woodland knight of Elven green,: 71.
"Beyond the edge, there lies the Silent Sea!: 74.
"Beyond the shadow of despair,: 66.
"Bitter is this heart of mine,: 5.
"Born out of legend long ago,: 72.
"Clouds melt into the sultry skies,: 30.
"Cú Chulainn, in his battle rage,: 52.
"Deirdre heard the voice of her loved one,: 20.
"Diaphanous rain fell in glistening torrents,: 25.
"Draco gazed upon the inauspicious stars,: 61.
"Eyes, crystalline composure mid the frosted frore,: 50.
"Fantasy, the Foreboding!: 49.
"Fires of passion, bon fires burn,: 12.
"Forged out of fables long ago,: 27.
"Four noble Queens of Avalon,: 64.
"Gazing upon the crystalline abyss,: 32.
"Gone is that land which once I knew,: 67.
"How fast can the dragon fly,: 33.
"In lands unfit for man nor beast,: 77.
"Isolde drains the cup of life,: 82.
"I tarry here alone,: 44.

RUNECASTER

"Lost is that lore,: 73.
"Oh beauteous beast, within thee hies,: 22.
"Oh Berengaria, my love!: 13.
Oh woe to the world,: 29.
Once, in legend long ago,: 6.
"Once upon a time,: 54.
"On Salisbury plain, at stark Stonehenge,: 55.
"Out of a time of darkness,: 28.
"Proud king of old, embattled bold,: 19.
"Proud queen of Celts,: 38.
"Rapunzel, Rapunzel, who can she be?: 3.
"Reflected thoughts of clouded dreams,: 24.
"Senach, in thy darkling cowl,: 78.
"She was the wife of Gorlois,: 31.
"Sparkling spritely, gleaming glitter,: 40.
Strewn with stars, the lunar nocturne,: 15.
Such fabled lore lies yet untold,: 68.
"The alembic of fancy,: 43.
"The counterfeit of thine affections,: 65.
"The intricacy of the written word,: 84.
Their mother sadly passed away,: 7.
"The Menhir nigh the mound,: 75.
"The moon beams bright mid darkling dell,: 9.
"The opal moon spread leprous light,: 37.
"The sun shone bright, that autumn dawn,: 35.
"The terebinthine frosted frore,: 56.
"The time of magic is at hand,: 45.
"The weirding wights of mounded downs,: 11.
"The wildcat's senses sharpen,: 79.
"They clashed so bravely,: 39.
"Though seasons balked at storm of war,: 76.
"To whom art thou behove,: 70.
"'Twas in the merry month of May,: 41.
"We, an ancient people are,: 58.
"Were ever lips so sweet as she,: 16.
"What fateful chance that she should stray,: 46.
"While not the darkling hours away,: 81.
"Whilst halls of Tara soft resound,: 23.
"Whilst thou art captive in my arms,: 48.
"Winsome as a wand,: 53.

95

RUNECASTER

"With frosting breath and eyes aflame,: 42.
"Within the lacustrine allure,: 47.
"Within the misted moon's repose,: 51.
"Word of invasion reached the king,: 57.

RUNECASTER

~CONTENTS~

RUNECASTER